GONDOLIN PRESS

I0203658

Paolo Pasqualucci

THE PARALLEL COUNCIL

The Anomalous Beginning
of the Second Vatican Council

gondolin press

THE PARALLEL COUNCIL – *Paolo Pasqualucci*

Original title: *Il Concilio Parallelo* (2014)

© Fede & Cultura (Italy)
www.fedecultura.com

© **gondolin press**

1331 Red Cedar Cir
80524 Fort Collins CO

www.gondolinpress.com
info@gondolinpress.com

2018 © Gondolin Institute LLC

ISBN 978-1-945658-12-9

First Italian edition: May 2014
First U.S. edition: December 2018

TO THE READER

This volume is a study I published in serial form in seven continuous issues of the anti-modernist journal "sì sì no no" in 2001 (XXVII), from n. 10 to n. 16, under the pseudonym Canonicus, according to the practice in use in that magazine by the will of its praiseworthy founder, Fr. Francesco Putti of the Roman clergy, who died in 1984. The study concerns the tumultuous and in a certain regard anomalous beginning of the Second Vatican Ecumenical Council, and the consequences this beginning had on the elaboration of a conciliar document of fundamental importance, namely the Constitution *Dei Verbum* on Divine Revelation, which I have chosen in preference to other conciliar documents, which however are no less important. I believe this study, until now largely unknown to the wider public and unique in its kind, is still capable of sparking the interest of those investigating into and reflecting on that Council, whose unusual pastoral attitude was certainly a *unicum* in the history of the Church, non conditioned by personal preference. This work is for those who wish to understand how the events actually took place, out of love for the Church but also for the truth.

I have completely revised the text and made various changes and additions. I have left the use of the "royal we" from the original draft. In the quotations, the words in square brackets are mine. In referencing the most recent literature I have used above all the history of Vatican II by Prof. Roberto De Mattei, who finally gave us a realistic picture of the unfolding of the Council. I realize that the essay deals with *technical* issues, as is commonly said: issues concerning regulations, deliberations, competence, procedures, problems of legality and legitimacy. An arid subject, which publishers are generally reluctant to publish because it is too specialized, even when exposed (as I believe I have done) in the clearest and simplest way possible. However, if Catholics who have remained faithful to the Tradition of the Church, to its perennial Magisterium, want to understand fully how things went at Vatican II, they cannot continue to leave this "more technical" subject in the hands of progressive historiographers who, in their various schools, have always represented it in such a way as to conceal negative facts and aspects that have abnormally influenced the course of the Council.

I thank Maria Caso, director in charge of "Sì sì no no", for having kindly consented to this new edition.

1.

THE BEGINNING OF THE SECOND VATICAN COUNCIL UNDER THE BANNER OF "DE-LEGITIMIZATION" AND THE VIOLATION OF LEGALITY

Foreword

The Constitution *Dei Verbum* on Divine Revelation is one of the shorter constitutions of Vatican II (only twenty-six articles) and yet one of the most important because of its subject. It was one of the most analyzed and discussed texts during Vatican II, and has continued to be so since then. The schema presented in the conciliar meeting hall, after the one elaborated by the Theological Commission was rejected in the preparatory phase, underwent a much debated development, so much so that the discussion dragged on until the end of the Council: from November 1962 to November 1965. And not only: the whole affair began with blatant infractions of "conciliar legality" (Amerio) and was carried out in a climate of crisis and delegitimization of the constituted authority. This essential aspect, still ignored by the official or prevalent historiography of Vatican II, has been highlighted in various ways, as is known, in the works of Fr. Wiltgen, Romano Amerio, and Msgr. Spadafora, and has been confirmed by historical writings since the mid-1990s. At the beginning of the twenty-first century, it was brought to the attention of a wider audience by the "unwritten" history of Vatican II of Prof. Roberto De Mattei.[1]

---

[1] RALPH. M. WILTGEN S.V.D., *The Rhine flows into the Tiber. A History of Vatican II*, Devon 1979, 1st ed. 1967; ROMANO AMERIO, *Iota Unum. Studio sulle variazioni della Chiesa Cattolica nel secolo XX*, Ricciardi, Milan-Naples 1986[2]; MONS. FRANCESCO SPADAFORA, *La tradizione contro il Concilio. L'apertura a sinistra del Vaticano II*, Rome 1989, reprint n.d. EDI. POL., Frosinone; ID., *La 'Nuova Esegesi'. Il trionfo del modernismo sull'Esegesi Cattolica*, Albano Laziale 1996 (which includes twenty-seven articles that appeared in "sì sì no no" under his name from 1993-1995). For our topic, see also ABBÉ MICHEL SIMOULIN, *Les vota des évêques en réponse à la consultation préparatoire au Concile Vatican II*, in: *Église et Contre-Église au Concile Vatican II, Actes du 2ème*

The purpose of this work is to bring out, possibly even more clearly than from the analyses of the aforementioned authors, both the violations of conciliar legality and the delegitimization of the constituted authority.

A strong wind of revolt

In the schema elaborated in the preparatory phase and then rejected, *Dei Verbum* was not entitled *De Divina Revelatione*, but more correctly *De Fontibus Revelationis*, since the Magisterium had always given equal weight to Sacred Scripture and Tradition.

There the centuries-old teaching of the Church was expounded with "total clarity": Apostolic Tradition and Sacred Scripture; divine inspiration; absolute inerrancy of the Sacred Books; the Gospels and

---

Congrès Théologique de "sì sì no no", Janvier 1996, Versailles 1996, pp. 75-110; ABBÉ PHILIPPE LOVEY, *Les schemas préparatoires,* Ibid., pp. 111-147. On the side of the "progressives", the documentation collected by ETIENNE FOUILLOUX, *Vatican II commence,* Univ. Cath. De Louvain, 1993. For the memoirs referred to in this text, we refer above all to MARIE-DOMINIQUE CHENU, *Diario del Vaticano II. Note quotidiane al Concilio 1962-1963,* tr. it. Il Mulino, Bologna 1966, with an ample and interesting introduction by A. Melloni. For the overview, in addition to the multilingual *Storia del Concilio Vaticano II,* 5 voll., 1995-2001, Il Mulino, Bologna – Peeters, Leuven, supervised by G. Alberigo, I kept in mind ROBERTO DE MATTEI, *Il Concilio Vaticano II. Una storia mai scritta,* Lindau, Torino 2010. The concise history of Fr. Wiltgen is always very useful, which first reconstructed objectively the true climate of Vatican II, showing the progressive and well-planned prevalence of the "liberal" (i.e., neo-modernist) faction. The diary and letters of Fr. Chenu, and the letters and diary passages of other protagonists, cited in the rich and valuable footnotes, amply document the frenetic activity of progressive theologians (several of which had already been formally censored or placed "*sub-iudice*" by Pius XII) in the lead-up to the Council and during its development, under the protective (and no less frenetic) wing of the cardinals of liberal-modernist tendencies (Frings, Döpfner, König, Liénart, Léger, Suenens, etc.). Moreover, they confirm the existence (at least since September 1962) of a resolute will to reject the first four schemas drawn up by the preparatory commissions, concerning the Dogmatic Constitutions (op. cit, p. 58, p. 65 n. 19). The theologians of "modernizing" tendencies, with the Swiss Hans Küng and the German Karl Rahner at the head, were among the first to propose their outright rejection.

their authors; their full historicity; the relationship between the Old and the New Testament; the teaching of the Holy Scripture.[2]

This schema, sent by the Central Theological Commission together with another six (the first out of a total of twenty constitution schemas) to all the bishops in the summer of 1962, three months before the opening of the Council, provoked a harsh reaction from the whole progressive front, whose leaders were mainly cardinals, bishops, and theologians from countries along the Rhine (Holland, Belgium, France, Germany, Austria, Switzerland). Hence the name "European Alliance" given to them by Fr. Wiltgen in his book, entitled with effective imagery: "The Rhine Overflows into the Tiber".[3] A key figure of this alliance, as is known, was the Belgian Dominican Edward Schillebeeckx, a theologian of the Dutch hierarchy, and later the main author of the famous and much-criticized "Dutch Catechism", which, according to the exegete Msgr. Spadafora, contained a full "fourteen major dogmatic errors".[4]

The seven schemas of the constitutions (the only ones completed at that point) addressed: "The Sources of Revelation"; "Keeping Pure the Deposit of Faith"; "The Christian Moral Order"; "Chastity,

---

[2] F. SPADAFORA, La 'Nuova Esegesi'. Il trionfo del modernismo sull'Esegesi Cattolica, op. cit., p. 159. Msgr. Spadafora assessment must be considered substantially correct. However, it should not be forgotten that in the preparatory commissions there were *novatores* among the experts (see below), which is why Cardinal Alfredo Ottaviani and Fr. Sebastiaan Tromp S.J, respectively president and secretary of the Theological Commission (see below), had to struggle to impose a *correct exposition* of the Church's doctrine. (On the work of the Theological Commission, we naturally kept in mind GIUSEPPE ALBERIGO (ed.), Storia del Concilio Vaticano II, vol. 1, pp. 242 ff, on the debate around De Fontibus, Ibid., pp. 327-329, and vol. 2, pp. 259 ff).

[3] R.M. WILTGEN, The Rhine flows into the Tiber, pp. 15-19. On the breadth of this reaction, which involved all the progressives, and on the undoubted existence of the "European Alliance", cf. M.-D. CHENU, Diario, cit., pp. 57-69. In Italy the Alliance enjoyed the support of Cardinals Lercaro and Montini (the latter in a more nuanced way).

[4] F. SPADAFORA, La 'Nuova Esegesi', op. cit., p. 159. The athletic and dapper Schillebeeckx has gone down in history as the destroyer of Catholicism, now practically extinct, in the Netherlands and Belgium, greatly assisted in the enterprise by Cardinal Suenens, another celebrated novator.

Marriage, Family and Virginity"; "The Sacred Liturgy "; "The Means of Communication"; "The Unity of the Church with the Eastern Churches".[5] The first four constitutions were conceived as Dogmatic Constitutions. The schemas on the deposit of faith and on the Christian moral order condemned numerous errors in the philosophical, theological, and moral fields, looking with concern upon the widespread signs of a moral decadence occurring throughout the West.

These subjects could not have pleased the modernizers. Schillebeeckx made a strong negative comment, which rejected all four of the first constitutions proposed. He saved only the fifth schema, that on the liturgy, the elaboration of which had involved also the progressives or liberals or neo-modernists or liberal-modernists or "modernizers", as you prefer (= novators), present in the preparatory commission.[6] This commentary was printed and distributed in a pamphlet to the Fathers who were beginning to flow into Rome for the Council and immediately individual Episcopal Conferences began to send petitions to the Presidency of the Council to postpone the discussion on the first four schemas, starting instead from the fifth, dedicated to the liturgy.

The first four schemas concerning the four Dogmatic Constitutions clearly exposed the traditional Catholic doctrine, which was also defended by denouncing and condemning multiple errors, in moderate but conceptually very clear language. As it should have been.

---

[5] JOSEPH KOMONCHAK, *La lotta per il concilio durante la preparazione*, in *Storia del Concilio Vaticano II*, 1, pp. 177-379; p. 252; pp. 433-434; R.M. WILTGEN, *The Rhine flows into the Tiber*, p. 23.

[6] R.M. WILTGEN, op. cit., p. 23. The term "novators" (*novatores*) was used during the Council by Cardinal Browne in attacking the substantially Protestant conception of the Mass that had worked its way into the schema on the Liturgy, cf. PH. LOVEY, op. cit., pp. 138-139, which is largely based on Fouilloux. Schillebeeckx also criticized the way the schemas were written, judging them "scholastic", a term which, among the progressives, expresses both their aversion to dogma and to Scholasticism (especially to St. Thomas, whom they for that matter refuse to study). On the "battle for the liturgy", extensively underway before the opening of the Council, see R. DE MATTEI, op. cit., pp. 181-187.

This, however, infuriated the novators, imbued with neomodernist *"nouvelle théologie"*. Schillebeeckx asked, albeit as a hypothesis, for the first four schemas to be *rewritten*. He did not like the proposed Dogmatic Constitutions because they were not sufficiently "pastoral" or "ecumenical"; in the terminology of progressive theologians: because they were "intellectual", "abstract", "theoretical"; because they "ignore the new world" and instead "limit themselves to denouncing intra-theological errors", thus appearing "doctrinal"; because "they have the tone of the decrees of Vatican I"; because they are "scholastic", etc.[7] He accused them of representing *only one* line of theological thought, as if this "direction" were not, instead, "the constant and immutable thought of the Church".[8]

The teaching of the Magisterium was artificially downgraded to being simply "Roman" theology, and in consequence was openly discussed and even rejected, since these theologians no longer wanted to hear about the two sources of Revelation. These critiques showed no particular originality of thought. However – and this is the point – their proponents justified themselves with the idea of that *ecumenical openness* which John XXIII had already repeatedly set as the foundation of the Council and which he then consecrated with the famous opening *Allocution* of October 11, 1962. The same refrain was repeated obsessively: the proposed schemas did not respect the "ecumenical directives" expressly provided by the Pope.

Thus, even before its official beginning, the Council was assailed by strong winds of revolt, which resulted in the request, by a pugnacious minority, to change the order of discussion that had been established with the Pope's approval and even to rewrite the schemas of the first four Dogmatic Constitutions. To fully understand the revolutionary significance of these demands, we must also consider things from a legal point of view.

Unfounded victimism

The pretensions and attitude of the novators were those of individuals making a show of having had their rights trampled by the Curia's manner of handling things, personified in their eyes by

---

[7] M.-D. CHENU, op. cit., pp. 57-59; p. 61, 62, 79.

[8] F. SPADAFORA, *La 'Nuova Esegesi'*, op. cit., p. 154.

Cardinal Ottaviani, prefect of the Congregation of the Holy Office and therefore official guardian of Catholic Doctrine, who had put before them the fait accompli of schemas not to their liking. But the Curia had not trampled on anyone's rights. An ecumenical council had rarely been prepared with greater scruple, conscientiousness and respect for the rights and opinions of all. The practice of Vatican I was followed, while improving and elaborating upon it.

The Council's preparation lasted three years. The *pre-preparatory phase* (one year) ended with sixteen volumes of roughly 10,000 pages, which gathered the opinions or *vota* of the bishops (about 3,000), the Faculties of Theology, the Congregations of the Curia and the analysis of the aforementioned opinions of the bishops. The *preparatory phase* (another two years) culminated on the eve of the Council with twenty schemas of constitutions and decrees elaborated by ten preparatory Commissions, which had worked under the supervision of a *Central Preparatory Commission,* whose president was naturally the Pope.[9] It was obvious that the members of the Curia predominated in the preparatory Commissions, since they were the most theologically competent and represented continuity in the teaching of the papal Magisterium. Also among them there were novators, such as Cardinals Bea and Tisserant.

The prodromes of "reconciliation" with error

Among the commissions, the most important was the *Theological Commission,* also called the *Doctrinal Commission* precisely because it dealt with doctrine, with dogma. It was necessarily chaired by Cardinal Ottaviani, since for several centuries it had been the Holy Office's task to watch over the purity of Catholic doctrine. Since almost all the matters addressed by the other commissions had doctrinal implications – which were the exclusive responsibility of the Theological Commission – whoever controlled the latter de facto controlled all the other commissions.

The *Theological Commission,* as we have said, already contained progressive elements in the preparatory phase. And not only among

---

[9] R.M. WILTGEN, pp. 19-22; R. AMERIO, § 29 (p. 43); M. SIMOULIN, op. cit., PH. LOVEY, op. cit.; *Storia del Concilio Vaticano II,* vol. 1, pp. 71ff; pp. 181 ff; R. DE MATTEI, pp. 118-196.

the cardinals who were part of it, but also among the *consultores*, theologians called to participate only as experts or consultants, in order to be able to use their knowledge in the elaboration of the schemas. In fact, Levillain notes, "a wide opening was made". Among the *consultores* "we noted the presence of the Fathers Congar, de Lubac, Hans Küng, etc. The whole team of theologians implicitly condemned by the encyclical *Humani Generis* in 1950 [by Pius XII] had been called to Rome by the will of John XXIII. The Council opened in an era of reconciliation..."[10] All the appointments of the members and consultants of the commissions, both preparatory and non-preparatory, were formally approved by the Pope. With the appointments of Congar and his companions, John XXIII, behind the screen of *openness*, in fact reconciled the Church with error, thus failing in his duties as Supreme Pontiff, since the theologians he had chosen had not been condemned only "implicitly." Some had been suspended from teaching and their books put on the Index; others were placed "*sub iudice*" by the Holy Office itself. Those theologians had reprinted some of their heterodox works with various modifications, but without altering the substance of their thought and without ever making amends for their errors. And very serious errors they were. One, for example, involved obscuring the distinction between the supernatural and human nature (de Lubac S.J.), an idea that contradicted the dogmas of original sin and the gratuitousness of grace, opening the way to the divinization of man. A related theory affirmed the notion of "anonymous Christians" (Karl Rahner S.J.), according to which, through the Incarnation Our Lord had already saved every man; all men thus were elevated "anonymously" to the rank of Christians without even knowing it! Salvation (which now became collective and pre-established for the whole human race as if it were included in human nature) no longer required the indispensable contribution of our free will, of the individual conscience of each man, of our daily personal sanctification, in short, of the intellect and will that invoke divine grace and cooperate with its action in us. The very meaning of the Church and its mission changed: it was no longer a matter of drawing souls from the darkness

---

[10] PHILIPPE LEVILLAIN, *La mécanique politique de Vatican II. La majorité et l'unanimité dans un concile*, Beauchesne, Paris 1975, p. 77.

of error and sin (since the Incarnation had already saved everyone!) but of convincing all men through "dialogue" to become aware of the salvation that had already occurred and to collaborate therefore with the Pope to realize (each one remaining in his own religion and belief) the Love of the Father in this world, the Kingdom of God on Earth by achieving the unity of humankind through universal peace. Fistfuls of the ancient pantheistic and millenarian heresies, wrapped in the multicolored vagaries of contemporary thought, were flung about by the "new theologians", imbued with modernism. And now the Pope himself was bringing such characters with full authority into a preparatory commission that was among the most delicate of the Council! This move by John XXIII, which caused considerable shock among conscious clergy and believers, must be considered in its proper light: it anticipated the Pope's subsequent attitude of *acquiescence* and *objective complicity* in the subversive action of the "European Alliance".

The first violations of legality

The novators, however, though well represented in the preparatory commissions, had managed only partially to advance the approach they desired and almost exclusively in the schema on the liturgy, that is, in only one of the five schemas that contained the fundamental teaching of the Church. Hence an angry reaction, which aimed to subvert what had been defined and accomplished *with the seal of legality*.

In fact, the first seven schemas, officially entitled *First Series of the Schemas of Constitutions and Decrees*, were sent to the council fathers around the world on July 13, 1962. In the *Acta Apostolicae Sedis* on that date, however, there is not formal decree of dispatch. There is nothing. It seems that the authorization to send the schemas was given by the Pope orally.

According to Fr. Wiltgen, "since these schemas were numbered in succession, most of the bishops thought that the intention was to discuss them in that order".[11]

---

[11] R.M. WILTGEN, p. 23.

The interpretation of the bishops certainly corresponded to the meaning of the Code of Canon Law then in force (issued in 1917), which arranged that the powers *exclusively* pertaining to the Pope before an Ecumenical Council were: to convoke it, to preside over it directly or *per alios*, "to establish and designate the subjects (*res*) that should be dealt with and the ordering (*ordinem*) to be observed"; to transfer the Council, suspend it, dissolve it, and confirm its decrees.[12]

The *res* mentioned presumably concerned matters that a Council was to address, according to the direction, the intention manifested by the Pope before even beginning the actual preparatory phase. The *ordo* to observe (*ordinem servandum*) referred with all evidence to the concrete order of the Council, in its various aspects, including the regulatory aspect, essential to the functioning of any assembly and therefore of the Council understood as a legal system, established and operating under the principle of legality (which, as such, includes that of legal certainty). This arrangement had its source solely in the Pope's supreme power of jurisdiction; in this case, the Pope had decided to gather the bishops in that ecclesiastically constituted body that is the Ecumenical Council. Therefore, when the Pontiff authorized the dispatch of the schemas of the First Series, in that order, numbered in that manner, it must be assumed that he had implicitly approved the order itself. The authorization, even if only verbal, showed that the Pope had officially made his own the order in which the schemas had been presented to him by the bodies of the preparatory phase, a phase that he had moreover meticulously controlled in his capacity as President of the Central Preparatory Commission. The bishops therefore found themselves faced with an order of the constitutions to be discussed that they could not change unless the Pope granted them his *placet* in this regard, reversing his own (official, not private – even if only oral) decision, which constituted the *concrete* legal order of

---

12 "*Eiusdem Romani Pontificis est Oecumenico Concilio per se vel per alios praeesse, res in eo tractandas ordinemque servandum constituere ac designare, Concilium ipsum transferre, suspendere, dissolvere, eiusque decreta confirmare*" (CIC 1917, c. 222 § 2). The *Codex iuris canonici* (CIC) of 1983 has maintained these prerogatives in can. 388. The powers referred to in the aforementioned can. 222 § 2 fall within those of the "supreme and full jurisdictional power over the whole Church", which belongs to the Pope by divine right, in this case as regards "the discipline and governance of the Church" (CIC 1917, can. 218 § 1).

the Council. The requests to change the order of discussion amounted to an open disavowal of the authority of the Pope, who had shown that he had made that order already by verbally authorizing the dispatch of the schemas to the bishops.

But the rebellious cardinals and bishops even demanded that the first four schemas (all doctrinal) be rewritten, which practically meant a rejection of the schemas, something which they later requested openly in the conciliar hall in the discussion on the *De Fontibus Revelationis* (see below). Was not such a request to be considered even more harmful to the papal authority?

The defenders of Tradition and of the prerogatives of the Apostolic See have maintained that the schemas sent were to be considered approved *as to their content* by the Pope, which would have made it impossible not only to reject them outright, but even to simply revise them in such a way that would essentially constitute a rejection of the initial schemas.

The justification of historiography "the bolognese way"

This thesis is still rejected by the novators and by the majority historiography, based on two arguments.

"Even if it is incorrect to state that the schemas had been approved by the Pope, this was the interpretation of the defenders of the schema, who were leaning on this argument to support the inadmissibility of a total refusal of the transmitted preparatory schemas in the conciliar hall for discussion. Cfr. the speeches by Ruffini (A/S I/3, p. 37), Quiroga y Palacios (p. 39), De Barros Câmara (p. 68), Fares (p. 85) etc. It was an argument that was perhaps effective for many, but lacking any foundation. In fact, the Pope's approval did not refer to the content of the schemas, but only to their transmission for discussion in the hall. It is precisely what was rightly pointed out in those days in a note produced by Lercaro's environment, which recalled the precedent of Vatican I and the apostolic letter of November 27, 1869, *Multiplices inter*, in which Pius IX specified that the schemas, previously drawn up by theologians and canonists, had been reserved *"nulla Nostra approbatione munita, intacta Patrum cognitioni"*.[13]

This is the *first argument*, which some wanted to justify on the precedent of the regulation issued by Pius IX for Vatican I: the schemas were sent to the Fathers without any preliminary pontifical approval (*"nulla Nostra approbatione munita"*) to be reserved "wholly intact for the Father's full knowledge".[14]

The *second argument* of progressive historiography is based on a provision of the Vatican II regulations. During the dramatic debate that preceded the sinking of the schema on the sources of Revelation, Cardinal Gilroy of Sydney, the current president, had replied polemically to Cardinal Ottaviani, who had reminded the Fathers that it was against canon law to reject a schema approved by the Pope; the former read, amid warm applause, art. 33 § 1 of the Council regulation which admitted precisely the possibility of the total rejection of any schema.[15]

The text was as follows: "Every Father can speak orally on any presented schema either by approving or rejecting it, and by modifying it, after having deposited a summary of his intervention at the General Secretariat at least three days prior".[16] The precedent established by Pius IX and the Vatican II regulations seemed therefore to disprove completely the defenders of Church Tradition, particularly Cardinal Ottaviani, a supreme canonist (whose *Institutiones Iuris Publici Ecclesiastici* constitutes a classic), who nevertheless was reprimanded here by the novators precisely on a point of law. Let us see how things were and how they are, starting with the first argument.

---

[13] *Archivio ISR, F-Alberigo II/5,* quoted in *Storia del Concilio Vaticano II*, vol. 2, p. 290 n. 86.

[14] We quote the *Rules of the Ecumenical Vatican Council I* from the bilingual edition which appeared in *La Civiltà Cattolica*, vol. III, series VII, pp. 676-696, under the heading *Cose spettanti al Concilio (Things pertaining to the Council)*. The quote is on p. 690.

[15] R.M. WILTGEN, pp. 48-49.

[16] Rules of the Second Vatican Ecumenical Council – *Ordo Concilii Oecumenici Vaticani II celebrandi*: AAS, LIV (1962) pp. 609-631. In art. 33 § 1 the text reads: *"Quivis Pater verba facere potest de unoquoque proposito schemate vel admittendo, vel reiciendo, vel emendando, suae orationis summa Secretario generali saltem tres ante dies scripto exhibita"*.

2

A SUBVERSIVE PRINCIPLE
IN THE VATICAN II REGULATIONS

Pius IX and the *ius proponendi*

How should we understand Pius IX's affirmation in art. VII of the regulations he issued for Vatican I?

The written regulations and the practice of having a schema drawn up by a preparatory commission to be discussed later in the council hall were introduced with Vatican I, to improve upon the procedure used at the Council of Trent. The freedom of discussion granted unlimited time for interventions, but limited the object of such interventions, because the regulations granted the Fathers neither the faculty to revise the schemas nor to reject them, even if the reform of February 20, 1870 had formally introduced the faculty of *amendment*, initially not provided for.[17] Granting bishops the faculty to reject a schema would have meant running the risk of effectively nullifying the *ius proponendi* in the Council, which rightfully belongs to the Supreme Pontiff, by virtue of his supreme jurisdiction over the whole Church.

Pius IX laid claim to this *ius proponendi* also in the act of granting the Bishops the right to present written proposals to perfect the schemas.

"Although the right and the office to propose [*ius et munus proponendi*] the matters to be treated in the holy ecumenical Synod, and to request the Fathers' opinions on these matters, belong solely to Us and this Apostolic See, nevertheless we not only desire, but even urge that, if some of the Council Fathers have anything to propose, which in their opinion can contribute to the public good, they may do so freely".[18] Then followed the instructions on how to present the eventual request: a written petition was needed, which had to concern

---

[17] For all these aspects see PH. LEVILLAIN, pp. 108-130.
[18] *Things pertaining to the Council*, pp. 680-681.

the common good of Christianity, explain its reasons, and not contain "anything alien from the constant sense of the Church, and from its inviolable traditions".[19] The petition had to be presented to an ad hoc commission (*Commissio de Postulatis*) which, after having discussed it "diligently", would submit its conclusions to the Pope, who would decide "with mature consideration" whether to admit it to the Synodal deliberation.[20]

In *Multiplices inter*, Pius IX therefore stated clearly that the right to propose or *ius proponendi* in the Council belonged only to the Pope. The Pope was not granting the bishops a *ius proponendi* equal to his own, nor giving them his own nor authorizing them to exercise it by proxy. He was simply *granting them the power to join him, under his control, in the exercise of this right*. A *faculty* is not a right and this can be seen from the fact that it does not give rise to any obligation either in a counterparty or in any third party, nor much less to a penalty, if its exercise is in any way impeded. It is then typical of a faculty to depend totally on the will of the person who grants it, as is evident in the case in question, where the bishop's petitions were subject to the judgement of an ad hoc commission and above all to the final and decisive judgement of the Pope for them to be admitted to discussion in the Council.

The concession made by Pius IX was codified in the CIC of 1917, in can. 226: "The Fathers can add other questions to those proposed by the Roman Pontiff, which have however been preliminarily approved by the authority that directs the Council (*praeses Concilii*)", this authority being constituted (ex can. 222 §2), by the Pope or by his representatives.[21] This procedure to present a written petition containing "other issues" was then repeated almost identically in art. 40 of the Vatican II regulations, but with a nuance concerning the reference to the "traditions" of the Church, which removed the adjective "inviolable".[22]

---

[19] Ibid, p. 681.

[20] Ibid.: "... *ut Nos deinde matura consideratione de iis statuamus, utrum ad Synodalem deliberationem deferri debeant*".

[21] The rule was revived in can. 338 § 2 of the 1983 CIC.

[22] The new proposals will be admitted only if, among other things, "*nihil contineant quod a constanti Ecclesiae sensu eiusque traditionibus alienum sit*" (art. 40 § 1c).

The question of preliminary approval

Having established this essential point, that the *ius proponendi* in the Council belongs only to the Pope and therefore Pius IX had neither recognized nor delegated it to the bishops, let us now consider the question of papal approval of the preliminary schema.

Art. VII of the Vatican I regulations governed the discussion of the schemas in the plenary sessions of the Council or "General Congregations of the Fathers". After having reminded all that the schemas had been prepared with the contribution of theologians and canonists from the Curia and from the entire Catholic world, "to make the treatment of things more rapid for the Fathers," the text went on: "therefore we wish and command that the schemas of the decrees and canons expressed and ordered by the aforementioned persons, which We, without approving them, have reserved wholly intact for the Fathers' appraisal, be submitted to the examination and judgement of the Fathers themselves gathered in the general congregation".[23] The schemas, therefore, had to be printed and distributed to the Fathers, so that they could study them well in order to "accurately understand what their judgement should be".[24] In the case of serious dissent that cannot be resolved in the course of the General Congregation, the schema, together with the alleged difficulties, would be submitted to the examination of the competent Deputation, which would distribute the printed conclusions to the Fathers, for a definitive vote in the general congregation.[25]

In such a context, how should we understand Pius IX's declaration that he did not bestow upon the schemas "Our approval"? The Pope ordered ("we wish and command") that the schemas be sent to the bishops and with this order authorized their circulation. Was he perhaps authorizing the transmission of texts that did not have his approval? Evidently not. It seems clear to us that the "*nulla Nostra approbatione munita*" referred to the pontifical approval of an act

---

[23] "... *hinc volumus et mandamus, ut schemata decretorum et canonum ab iisdem viris expressa et redacta, quae Nos, nulla Nostra approbatione munita, integra integre Patrum cognitioni reservavimus, iisdem Patribus in Congregationem generalem collectis ad examen et iudicium subiiciantur*" (*Things pertaining to the Council*, p. 690).

[24] Ibid., p. 691.

[25] Ibid., p. 692.

pronounced *in a specific form*, that is formal, official, *final*, equipped with certain formulas or expressions that qualify it as such and make it unmodifiable by anyone.

It is evident that the pontiff could not affix this kind of seal of approval to the schemas to be sent to the bishops. He could not do so, above all from a logical point of view, for the simple reason that no bishop could have discussed a document formally approved in a definitive way (*in a specific form*) by the Pope. An approval of this kind conferred upon the schemas would have rendered vain the very purpose of the Ecumenical Council, which was to ensure that the Pope in the Council solemnly issued, with the approval of the bishops – of the bishops *together with the Pope* – certain, particularly important documents of the Magisterium. This is clear from the formula of the final approval of the conciliar decrees, given in art. VIII of the regulations of Pius IX: "The decrees now read [in solemn public congregation] pleased [*placuerunt*] all the Fathers [who had already approved them in their general congregations], with none rejecting them or (if perhaps some rejected them) except such and such a number, and We [the Pope], approving the sacred Council [*sacro approbante Concilio*], so we decree, establish and sanction them, as they were read"[26].

Therefore Pius IX, wishing for the bishops summoned to discuss *freely* the schemas of Dogmatic Constitutions he had had prepared, made it clear that the schemas had not been approved, that is, made his own, by the Pope *alone*, since he wanted them to be appropriated by the Ecumenical Council, that is by himself and all the bishops gathered by him with him in an extraordinary and solemn body of the Magisterium.

However, an *implicit* approval by the Pope *of the contents* of the schemas must be supposed: *the approval of their conformity to the deposit of faith*. The Pope's power of jurisdiction is based on the divine constitution of the Church because it belongs to him "by divine right"

---

[26] "*Decreta modo lecta placuerunt omnibus Patribus, nemine dissentiente; vel (si qui forte dissenserint) tot numero exceptis; Nosque, sacro approbante Concilio, illa ita decernimus, statuimus atque sancimus, ut lecta sunt*" (*Things pertaining to the Council*, p. 694).

from the moment he accepts his election to the Sacred Throne.[27] Now this "authentically episcopal, ordinary and immediate"[28] power is conferred principally "to confirm the brothers in faith" (Lk 22:32) through the care and maintenance of the deposit of faith, the supreme *duty* of the Pope before God and the whole Church. This command of Our Lord, like others, is always in effect and at no time can the Pope withdraw from it. For this reason, it is the *duty* of the Pope to control the merits of documents such as the dogmatic (and non-dogmatic) schemas of an ecumenical council, to assess their conformity to the deposit of faith. It is not necessary that this duty be stated by any rule of positive law, since the norm established in this regard by Our Lord Jesus Christ, the dictate of Revelation witnessed by the Gospels, suffices.

One must therefore conclude that Pius IX's approval to transmit the schemas excluded both a *specific* approval of their content and that formal and final approval that the Pope wanted to confer upon them with the bishops in the Council called by him for this purpose. However, it implied in itself an implicit pontifical approval of their dogmatic content (theological and canonistic), judged by the Pope to conform to the deposit of faith. Otherwise he would have carefully avoided authorizing their transmission.

A subversive faculty

We believe that it was this last type of approval that Cardinal Ottaviani was referring to when he claimed that a total rejection of the preparatory schemas was inadmissable. These schemas had received the Pope's approval not only to be circulated in the conciliar hall, but also as to their content, which was to be considered implicitly judged by him to conform to dogma (otherwise he would not have circulated them). Ottaviani rightly claimed that *rejecting* a constitutional schema, and a dogmatic one at that, whose content the Pope had implicitly approved (approval deduced from his order to send it to the bishops) meant going against canon law, because it demonstrated a rejection of the Pope's power of jurisdiction. The rejection of the

---

[27] CIC 1917 can. 219. The parenthetical phrase "*iure divino*" is missing in the corresponding norm of the CIC 1983, in can. 331.

[28] CIC 1917 can. 218 § 2; CIC 1983 cans. 331 and 332 § 1.

schema, in short, was already a form of rebellion against the Pope, with serious theological implications. It should be noted that the possibility for bishops to reject a schema *was not provided for* in the regulations of Vatican I. It would have appeared in contradiction with the primacy of Peter, with the free fulfillment of his duty to "confirm the brethren in faith". And in fact we saw how the neo-modernists, during Vatican II, knew how to take advantage of the faculty to reject the schemas, granted them by the regulations, to create a shift in opinion towards the rejection and total revision of the schemas (see above).

On the other hand, the Vatican I regulations granted the bishops a limited freedom of discussion. The text, as we have seen, stated that the schemas would be sent to the bishops so that they "would carefully understand what their judgement should be [*et quid sibi sententiae esse debeat, accurate pervideant*]" (art. VII, cit.); they were to understand, in essence, what contribution they should give, what the Pope expected of them, how they should vote: in a way, that is, to perfect the text, if necessary. The schemas concerned dogma: the definition of the doctrine of faith, primacy and papal infallibility. They were sent by the Pope, who had evidently found them in conformity with the deposit of faith and expressing sound and common doctrine, otherwise he would not have authorized their sending: with what justification would a bishop have rejected them? Would such an act also not have meant the rejection of the truths of faith, all or some, contained in these schemas? Could the Pope authorize regulations that would allow such a thing? He could not.

And in fact art. VII of the Vatican I regulations clearly shows, in our opinion, the papal *mens* in this regard. The text does not state that the schemas would allow the bishops to "understand accurately how they would *like* to vote" but how "they *should* vote". And how should they? In the only possible way, that indicated by St. Vincent of Lerins in chap. 23 of his *Commonitorium* (AD 434) on the "progress of the dogma and its conditions". In such a way as not to change it, not to alter it, but to deepen it without modifying it, preserving its specific nature; in short, according to the famous phrase: *"in eodem scilicet dogmate, eodem sensu, eademque sententia"*.[29] Admitting discussion to the

---

[29] *Ench. Patr.*, 2174.

ecumenical council up to the point of being able to reject *en bloc* schemas drawn up by theologians and canonists chosen by the Pope and substantially, even if not definitively, approved by the Pope, would in effect transfer the *ius proponendi* from the Pope to the bishops and open the door to the irruption of confusion, ambiguity and even error. Something which then promptly occurred in Vatican II.

3.

The Pope's surrender to the novators' requests

An invalid rule

Cardinal Ottaviani's highlighting in the Council of the inadmissibility of completely rejecting the schemas elaborated in the preparatory phase and transmitted to the bishops with the approval of the Pope was therefore to be considered extremely accurate, in our opinion. His emphasis shows that art. 33 § 1 of the Vatican II regulations, conferring on the bishops the faculty to reject the schemas in their entirety, conferred on them a real power of censorship over the schemas and therefore was in contradiction with canon law. And not only with canon law, since the Petrine *munus* "to confirm the brethren in the faith" – nullified by that *facultas reiciendi* – belongs to the divine constitution of the Church.

It must therefore be noted that John XXIII, by issuing the Vatican II regulations, had allowed a rule to be issued that would be harmful to the papal *auctoritas* and a source of contradiction. A rule that should have been considered invalid due to its manifest incompatibility with canon law and the divine constitution of the Church. Given the impossibility (or inappropriateness) of challenging regulations approved by the Pope, the rule at least should not have been applied. And the Fathers faithful to Tradition, in their interventions, essentially aimed at this, naturally without success.

The meticulousness of John XXIII
in the preparatory phase of the Council

At this point one may ask whether John XXIII had realized the subversive principle contained in art. 33 § 1 of the regulation he promulgated, as he wrote, "taking into account the particular nature and circumstances of this Council".[30] To verify this, we must look at the facts. And what do the facts show? That the Pope had followed *meticulously* (as was his duty, after all) all the preparation of the Council.

It was John XXIII himself who wanted his meticulousness to be documented. Let us consider the Apostolic Letter *Superno Dei Nutu* of June 27, 1960, with which he established the preparatory commissions. In that text, the Pope recalled the work done by the Ante-Preparatory Commission, which he constituted on May 17, 1959 and which had worked for a whole year to gather the "*consilia et vota*" of all the bishops, the opinions of the dicasteries of the Curia and of the "ecclesiastical and Catholic" universities.[31] And, perhaps to dispel any possible misunderstanding on the actual paternity of the direction of the Council, John XXIII specified: "We have followed all these investigations and these works ourselves with diligence and have considered what is proper to our office [of the Supreme Pontiff] to study assiduously and with the greatest attention [*Nostroque duximus muneri attentissime pervalutare*] the volumes containing the advices and the suggestions of the bishops, the proposals and warnings of the Sacred Dicasteries of the Roman Curia, the votes and the opinions of the Universities".[32] John XXIII had, therefore, read everything and evaluated everything and not as a private person but in the exercise of his papal power. In fact, he wanted to point out that it was part of the Pope's duties to exert an accurate control of the documents of the pre-preparatory phase and that he had carried out this control with the utmost diligence and scrupulousness. And in fact, the texts of these documents in the Pope's possession are full of notes in the margin, demonstrating a careful reading. From them it appears that John XXIII had found all the documents to his liking, except for some passages of the constitution's schema on the liturgy.[33]

Let us now see how John XXIII defined the essential tasks of the *Central Preparatory Commission* (*Commissio centralis*) presided over by himself, directly or "*per alios*": "The task (*munus*) of the Central Commission is to follow the work of the individual commissions and

---

[30] Apostolic Letter *Appropinquante Concilio*, 10. 8. 1962, in AAS (LIX) 1962, p. 611.

[31] AAS (LII) 1960, pp. 433-434.

[32] Ibid., p. 434.

[33] On this point cf. R. DE MATTEI, p. 235.

to give them, if necessary, a specific order, and to report their conclusions to Us, after having duly examined them [*rite perpensas*], so that We ourselves [*Nosmetipsi*] may establish [*statuamus*] the things that must be treated [*res... tractandas*] in the Ecumenical Council".[34]

What is of interest here to note, is the fact that the conclusions of the individual commissions, once examined by the Central Commission, were transmitted by the latter to the Pope, its president, so that he could *establish* [*statuere*] what was to be "treated in the Council". The Pope's task was certainly not understood here, on the part of the Pope himself, as that of a body that merely took note of the commissions' work revised by the Central Commission, to then transmit it to the council chamber without judging it on its merits. The text shows how the Pontiff did not identify himself with the Central Commission, but maintained an independent and superior position with respect to it, since it was not that Commission with the Pontiff as its president, but the Pontiff *alone* who would "establish" what should be addressed in the Council. This interpretation is also justified by the terminology used: "... *ad Nos deferre, ut res in Concilio Oecumenico tractandas Nosmetipsi statuamus*": "So that We ourselves might establish the things that must be addressed in the Council". The use of the reinforcing term (*Nosmetipsi* instead of *Nos*), which means "ourselves", and therefore "we ourselves", shows how the Pope wanted to emphasize the fact that, at the end of the whole process, he alone would establish what should be addressed in the Council. *Statuere*, to establish, is a verb that has a strong, precise meaning. It contains the idea of being on a solid foundation and, in a figurative sense, that of establishing by ordering or judging. This last idea seems to apply to our context, so that the concept affirmed in the quoted text appears to be the following: it is up to the Supreme Pontiff (*Nosmetipsi*) to establish and then judge which things should be discussed in the Ecumenical Council.

The formula used by Giovanni XXIII was perfectly in line with art. VII of the Vatican I regulations, in which Pius IX reiterated, as we have seen, the exclusive papal prerogative of the *ius proponendi* in the Council. In the apostolic letter that established the preparatory commissions of Vatican II, John XXIII only reaffirmed the same

---

[34] AAS (LII) 1960, p. 436.

principle. And he did so by describing the pontifical exercise of the *ius proponendi* with the expression "res in Concilio tractandas statuere", since this right is nothing other than a "deciding which things should be addressed in the Council". The affirmation of "establishing by judging" also contains the idea of the *approval on the merits* of what is judged and its authorization to proceed further; in other words, it contains the implicit approval of its dogmatic correctness as an unavoidable condition of the authorization to proceed further, to receive final and formal approval at the end of the specific debate in the Council.

The unsustainability of the novators' thesis and of progressive historiography

It therefore seems entirely unfounded to want to continue to support, as does the media-dominant progressive historiography, that "the Pope's approval did not refer to the content of the schemas",[35] as if the Pope's work in this delicate matter could have been reduced to a mere notarial function and had not already expressed itself in a clear *judgement* on the suitability of the schemas to continue their process until the Council. The thesis of the neo-modernists and of the prevailing historiography appears, in any case, irreconcilable with the dictates of the two regulations, those of Vatican I and Vatican II.

Our interpretation also seems to be confirmed by the actual development of the works of the preparatory phase. This is seen, for example, from the Report attached to the schema of the Dogmatic Constitution *De Fontibus Revelationis*, which Cardinal Ottaviani had read in the conciliar hall at the time of his presentation: "In the Central Commission, the text of the constitution was again revised, overall and in detail. By order of the Supreme Pontiff, the Theological Commission [which had drawn up the schema] had to respond to the findings made in the central commission. Finally, the commission of the most eminent Fathers charged with scrutinizing the amendments, having examined the issues, established the text to be proposed in the Council".[36] From this account we can deduce that the Pope, having

---

[35] *Storia del Concilio Vaticano II*, 2, p. 290 n. 86.

[36] The subcommittee on amendments had been created within the Central Commission itself, see *Storia del Concilio Vaticano II*, 1, pp. 321-329.

read the findings of the Central Commission, which he found evidently relevant *in its contents*, intervened in the procedure according to the regulation, when he ordered the Theological Commission to reply, which led to amendments, which, having been examined, led to the final text to be proposed in the Council; this text was judged by the Pope suitable to be presented in the conciliar hall.

Moreover, even the progressive historiography is forced to recognize here the existence of an assessment of merit (and therefore of a *judgement on the merits*) on the part of the Pope: "Of the three functions assigned to the central commission, the critical revision of the prepared texts was the only one performed accurately. Its task was to establish whether the prepared schemas were *suitable to be proposed to the Pope, whose judgement would have decided their presentation to the Council*".[37]

But even for the pre-preparatory activity, that historiography is forced to recognize the existence of a *judgement of merit* on the part of the Pope. "On July 9, however, the secretary of the ante-preparatory committee sent to the designated presidents the *"Quaestiones commissionibus praeparatoriis Concilii Vatican Oecumenici II positae"*, approved by the Pope on the 2nd, not without leaving them room for manoeuvering...".[38] Even here the approval of the Pope was certainly not a simple authorization to send the *Quaestiones*!

The acquiescence of John XXIII

Having clarified all this, let us take up again the thread of the discourse. The requests made by the novators, from the beginning of the Council, to reverse the order of the schemas to be discussed, to rewrite them, to withdraw them altogether, were therefore *intrinsically inadmissible*, because they specifically contradicted the *ius proponendi* of the Supreme Pontiff. In a broader sense, they were contrary to canon law and to the ecclesiastical and divine constitution of the Church. For the Pope to yield to such requests would have meant compromising his authority, resulting in a serious loss of prestige of

---

[37] *Storia del Concilio Vaticano II*, 1, p. 321. The underlining is ours.

[38] Ibid., 1, p. 164, in chap. II, *La fase ante-preparatoria (1959-1960). Il lento avvio dell'uscita dall'inerzia*, pp. 71-176.

the papal institution. And this, as we know, is precisely what happened.

The Presidency of the Council was not competent to change on its own initiative the order of the schemas to be discussed, as requested by the novators; it was only competent to receive the petitions in this sense and to serve as their interpreter, if necessary, with the Pope. In fact, on October 14, the Pope granted his *placet* to the request for reversal of the order of the schemas to be discussed, after receiving the ten cardinals of the Presidency. The decision was officially announced on October 15: the discussion would begin with the fifth schema, that on the liturgy, and no longer on the first, on the sources of Revelation.[39]

One cannot speak here of a *formal* violation of legality, because it was within the powers of the Pope to grant a change to the order of discussion that he had officially established. However, the legitimacy of the Council system was affected because the set of rules established by the forms of law by the legitimate authority, and therefore itself legitimate, was altered by a formally legitimate decision, nonetheless invalidating the authority itself (that of the papacy as an institution) that was the basis of that system. It invalidated it because the Pope accepted and made his own the revolutionary request of the novators, subversive of that authority and that order. The legitimacy of the Council system rested, in fact, both on the principle of legality and on the principle, also unwritten, that this system was based on an authority – that of the Pope – that would defend and maintain its integrity. Thus the papal acquiescence to the subversive demands of the novators effectively removed that legitimacy from that set of rules.

A serious precedent

This was able to happen also because, two days earlier, on October 13, there had been an open violation of the "conciliar legality" by

---

[39] R.M. WILTGEN, p. 24. It does not seem that the majority of the ten cardinals were in favor of the inversion; certainly the novators in the commission supported it; they were numerically equivalent to the defenders of Tradition, but more determined and aggressive, according to what we are given to understand.

Cardinal Achille Liénart of Lille, so well grasped by Romano Amerio and knowingly ignored by the majority conformist and progressive historiography, until the book of Prof. De Mattei, who gave it due importance.[40] An open and above all successful violation.

It occurred at the first session of the Council, where it was only necessary for the Assembly to elect sixteen members (out of twenty-four) for each of the ten conciliar commissions. The *Council Commissions*, said the regulations, "amend and prepare, according to the opinion expressed by the Fathers during the General Congregations, the schemas of the decrees and the canons".[41] All the bishops were eligible. The Curia, however, had also provided a list of experts, mostly already employed in the preparatory commissions, which could not have been to the liking of the novators. Congar, one of their leading elements, thus records the fact in his bilious *Mon journal du Concile*. "At the end of the ceremony this morning [it was the solemn opening of October 11], they distributed to the bishops an envelope containing: sheets to elect 16 of them in each of the ten commissions; a brochure with the complete and updated list of the Catholic episcopate; the list, divided by commissions and in a format similar to the ballot papers for the vote, of the bishops who were part of the preparatory commissions. It is an invitation to elect them... It is desirable that there be a certain continuity between the work of the Council and those of the preparatory commissions. But it is equally desirable that we now do something else better than what has been prepared: something pastoral, less scholastic... ".[42]

Even the ultra-progressive Congar, therefore, admitted the legitimacy of the procedure adopted by the Curia. But it is clear that for novators it was not a question of method but of substance. What they did not like was the *quality* of the work done by the committees, considered "too scholastic", a term that in the language of *nouvelle théologie*, as we have seen, contemptuously designated the patrimony of concepts with which the Magisterium has expounded and defended over the centuries the deposit of faith. It was therefore

---

[40] R. DE MATTEI, chap. III, pp. 197-283; pp. 203-206.

[41] Art. 5. The members to be appointed by the Pope were then brought to nine by John XXIII himself, who thus elevated the members of each commission to the number of 25.

[42] Cited in the *Introduction* to M.-D. CHENU, pp. 37-41.

necessary to do "something else and something better", something "pastoral", and in order to achieve this, it was necessary to prevent the scheduled voting and to ensure a majority in the committees to be constituted.

Therefore, on that fatal October 13, while Msgr. Felici, Secretary of the Council, was explaining the procedure to be followed, Cardinal Liénart, one of the members of the Presidency, unexpectedly stood up and asked for the floor, interrupting the speaker. The first president of the Council (first because he was the eldest), Cardinal Tisserant, who presided over the congregation, denied it to him in accord with the regulations, because the congregation had met to vote and not to decide whether to vote. The French prelate then grabbed the microphone and said, apparently: "*Excusez-moi, je vais la prendre quand-même* [Excuse me, I'll take it anyway]". And he read, to the applause of a part of the assembly, a declaration in which he asked that the vote be postponed and the Episcopal Conferences be allowed time to consult on the suitability of the candidates. Obviously, he wanted to have time to propose new lists of candidates. Liénart's request was supported by Cardinal Frings also on behalf of cardinals König and Döpfner and was accepted, after feverish consultations, by Cardinal Tisserant, who had just made the attempt (but only that) to apply the regulations to the illegal action of his colleague.[43]

---

[43] R.M. WILTGEN, pp. 16-17; R. AMERIO, § 41, pp. 74-75, who reproached Fr. Wiltgen for not having understood the illegality of the French Cardinal's gesture (Ibid., p. 75, note 12); PH. LEVILLAIN, pp. 185 ff; PH. LOVEY, p. 143. Levillain does not express any judgement, while noting that Cardinal Liénart, as a member of the Council Presidency, did not have the right to ask for the floor, since voting was under way (pp. 191-192). In any case, this author demonstrates the unreliability of the subsequent claim of the 78-year-old Cardinal Liénart that he had acted out of a sudden inspiration of the Holy Spirit. His speech was feverishly prepared in the preceding days, on the initiative of the then Msgr. Garrone, a Frenchman, after repeated meetings with different personalities. The "schema" of the intervention, prepared materially in Latin by Msgr. Garrone and three French priests, was given to cardinal Joseph Lefebvre (not to be confused with his more famous cousin, Msgr. Marcel Lefebvre) on the night between October 12th and 13th and he gave it the next morning to Liénart, who learned it by heart as he was driven to St. Peter's on the morning of the 13th, the day of the vote (pp. 188-190). Anything but the Holy Spirit! It was a

Confirming the seriousness of the episode, which cannot and must not be forgotten, we recall the words written by Cardinal Siri in his diary: "It is difficult to express the bewilderment and discomfort created by this affair. The participants dispersed in an air of evident and agitated malaise".[44] In contrast, heartfelt approval was expressed to Fr. Chenu, in a private meeting, by the two Protestant "monks" of the ecumenically varicolored community of Taizé, Schutz and Thurian, present at the Council as official observers: the "*Non serviam*" manifested unexpectedly in the conciliar hall from the very first session and at the very top of the Catholic hierarchy, could only have filled the sons of Luther with satanic satisfaction.[45]

Omissions and concessions of John XXIII

As soon as this important victory was achieved, as early as the afternoon of October 13, at a meeting of the ten members of the Council Presidency, Cardinals Frings, Liénart and Alfrink insisted that the order of the discussion of the schemas be reversed, which, as we mentioned above, the Pope granted them the following day.[46] It is therefore legitimate to consider that the manifest and above all fruitful violation of the legality perpetrated by Cardinal Liénart had somewhat corroborated the desire of the novators to persevere in their subversive intentions against the Council system.

John XXIII, who, according to what he wrote in his diary (the famous *Journal of a Soul*), was following every phase of the Council live from his studio thanks to an ad hoc radio link, was perfectly informed of everything.[47] He would certainly have been able to intervene, and

---

matter of the well-coordinated action of a lobby, which prepared the blow quickly but delivered it in cold blood. For more details, taken from the memoirs, see R. De Mattei, op. cit., pp. 203-206. Msgr. Garrone, later a cardinal, applied with great zeal the directives of the Council to the reform of French seminaries, destroying them completely. In the early 1950s, around one thousand priests were ordained in France each year; in 2006, 98 were ordained, not to mention the teaching received.

[44] Quoted in M.-D. CHENU, p. 72 n. 42.

[45] Ibid., p. 72.

[46] R.M. WILTGEN, p. 24.

[47] See M.-D. CHENU, p. 80 n. 62.

indeed *should have* intervened against the Presidency of the Council to reverse the decision and restore the legality violated by Cardinal Liénart and by the Presidency itself, which, according to the regulations, should not have even discussed the illegitimate appeal of the French cardinal. The Pope's institutional duty, as guarantor and defender of the *ordo* that he issued, was also to impose, where appropriate, respect for legality, using the methods established by the law to force the Presidency of the Council to restore the vote foreseen in the regulations. But John XXIII did not defend the conciliar legality. He let it go, and indeed the day after the coup of October 13 he yielded again, as mentioned, with a concession (the reversal of the order of discussion) no less serious than his failure to intervene in support of the sabotaged legitimate voting. In fact, thanks to that new concession, the novators had time to elaborate alternative schemas to those of the preparatory commission and to circulate them.

The triumph of illegality

In just three days, the novators had succeeded in obtaining from John XXIII, and without particular effort, the postponement of the election of commissions (from October 13th to the 16th) and the reversal of the order of matters to be dealt with. An authentic triumph: illegality paid. Then, in the elections, the novators obtained 49% of the available seats. They came to conquer half of the Theological Commission and to have a majority in that on the liturgy. This result was made possible also by the fact that on the very day of the proclamation of the results (October 20) John XXIII had let it be known, by the mouth of Msgr. Felici, that he had suspended the application of art. 39 of the regulation, which required an absolute majority (half plus one) to be elected, thus allowing the adoption of the criterion of the relative majority (that of the candidate who, without achieving an absolute majority, had received the highest number of votes). Thanks to this criterion, any majority, even a minimal one, was sufficient to be elected. Making this change to the regulations *"vivae vocis oraculo"* (i.e. verbally), a somewhat relaxed procedure, John XXIII made it known that he had accepted a suggestion from the Presidency of the Council.[48]

Even the famous monk Giuseppe Dossetti, an expert and advisor to Cardinal Lercaro at the Council, a left-wing Catholic, former president of the Christian Democrats, former parliamentarian, former professor of canon law (he was one of the architects of the current Constitution of the Italian Republic), in a memorandum, entitled *Remarks and proposals on the Council regulations*, deplored the climate of anarchy and substantial illegality that had been established since the beginning of the Council: "... we can understand that in the first few weeks some adjustments to the regulations have been necessary and future experience may suggest others [a touching up of the regulations was also done during Vatican I]. But it is of paramount importance that the modifications do not take place almost daily, but only in increasingly rare occasions, and above all that they do not take place in an informal way with decisions given '*vivae vocis oraculo*' but only in a formal way with well-thought-out and organic written rules". It should be emphasized that the "almost daily" and "informal" changes in the procedure were caused by novators' illicit pressure on the Council, to take control of its mechanisms and to modify its procedures to their advantage.[49]

An example of sweetened historiography

It seems useful to present the page of the *Brief History of Vatican II* by Giuseppe Alberigo, intended for the general public, in which the historian deals with the beginning of the conciliar work.

---

[48] R.M. WILTGEN, p. 18. In his diary, Chenu writes, on the date of October 20th: "The fathers are entering the session [to start work] without knowing yet whether the Pope, modifying the law, will decide for a single round with a relative majority, or if he will keep it for a second round, in view of an absolute majority. Without any deliberation, Felici gave the results of the first round, with the immediate election of sixteen members, with only a relative majority. The votes range from 1,800-1,700 to 700, and even less in many cases" (M.-D. CHENU, pp. 79-80).

[49] The Dossetti passage comes from M.-D. CHENU, pp. 101-105 n. 110, quotation on p. 102.

"Immediately [after the Opening Allocution of John XXIII, October 11, 1962] the Council Fathers concentrated on the election of commissions, i.e., working groups. The election would have offered a first opportunity to evaluate the consistency of the groups in which the assembly was organized. On the initiative of some European cardinals (the French Liénart and the German Frings) on October 13, the scheduled elections were postponed that same day, so that there was time to initiate contacts among the fathers, avoiding the otherwise inevitable confirmation of the preparatory commissions [that had elaborated the numerous schemas to be discussed in the conciliar hall, in three years of intense work].

The initiative [of the request for postponement] aroused surprise and emotion because it constituted the first warning of a conciliar conscience of the assembly that, despite being composed in overwhelming majority by persons "unprepared" for the mechanics of the assembly proceedings, was not passively deferring to the decisions made by the preparatory bodies. Thus the commissions were elected, but only on October 16, on the basis of lists prepared by the various episcopal conferences. The outcome was a clear prevalence of Central-European bishops and bishops from other continents compared to the 'Latin' bishops (Italians and Spaniards). Many of the participants in the preparatory commissions were not elected [just as the promoters of the coup d'état that led to the postponement wanted].

When the results were made known, it was also known that Pope John had made an exception to the rule, so that the fathers who had obtained the highest number of votes were elected for each committee, and not only those who had achieved an absolute majority; it was an unequivocal act of respect for the will of the assembly".[50]

From this reconstruction the illegality of the gesture made by Cardinal Liénart has been carefully expunged. It then gives an *entirely mistaken* interpretation of the "surprise and emotion" aroused by the gesture of the French cardinal. These sentiments were provoked above all by the unprecedented audacity that the gesture itself

---

[50] G. Alberigo, *Breve storia del Concilio Vaticano II*, Il Mulino, Bologna 2005, p. 46 (*Brief History of Vatican II*, Orbis Books, 2006).

revealed, from the sudden sensation that there was something wrong at a very high level, that of "eminences"; not from the perception "of the first warning of a conciliar conscience of the assembly", which would not have even be formed afterwards in the sense intended by Prof. Alberigo. A much more accurate representation of the effective feelings of the majority is the observation of Cardinal Siri quoted above, on the general bewilderment caused by the unfortunate episode. Or the apparently ironic one of Msgr. Luigi Borromeo, bishop of Pesaro, who wrote in his diary: "And so three thousand people endured the discomfort of going in the rain to St. Peter's to be told that the three thousand bishops do not know each other and that they had to go home to get to know each other a little." It was only the neo-modernist minority who recorded the event with enthusiasm, as evidenced by the memories of Cardinal Suenens, one of its leaders: "A happy twist and an audacious violation of the regulations! [...] In large part the fate of the Council was decided in that moment. John XXIII was pleased".[51] As the work of Prof. De Mattei has shown convincingly, the vast "center" of the conciliar assembly, judging by the *vota* cast by the bishops in the preparatory phase of the Council, was not particularly inclined to "openness". In the struggle that immediately arose in the Council between the two limited groups of novators and defenders of the Tradition of the Church, who had already faced off in the preliminary phase, this center allowed itself to be influenced by the more motivated group, the one better endowed with means of pressure, including external pressure, that is, by the progressive group, which was supported moreover by the spirit of the age, which pressured the Council with the media. For our part, we add that the "center" tried above all to understand towards which side the Pope was inclining, who (the Pope) was always the fundamental reference point for the overwhelming majority. Prof. De Mattei rightly notes that the progressive minority began to feel "for the first time to be the majority" only after the Pope sanctioned the rejection of the schema

---

[51] R. DE MATTEI, op. cit., p. 205, for both citations. The note by Suenens shows us a Pope clearly aligned with the progressive faction.

on the sources of Revelation and all the preparatory work (see below). And the "center" obviously began immediately to take it into account.[52]

Prof. Alberigo is silent also on the fundamental concession to invert the order of discussion, an essential concession in the novators' plan, closely connected (as we have just seen) to the request to postpone the vote. Regarding the oral adoption, in the conciliar hall, even *after* the results of the voting, of the criterion of the pure majority (an abnormal way of proceeding, stigmatized even by Dossetti, Alberigo's teacher), the latter is unable to say anything other than the adoption of that criterion, and *done in that way*, "was an unequivocal act of respect for the will of the assembly"! In reality, what was accepted was the suggestion of the Presidency of the Council, in which body, as we have seen, the novators had already succeeded in imposing themselves: on this detail our historian is silent. Of this suggestion, the *Brief History* makes no mention. The "conciliar conscience" of the "event" or *Erlebnis-Council*, fabricated by the historiography of a progressive matrix ("Bolognese" and non-Bolognese) as a fundamental hermeneutical category to understand the so-called "spirit of the Council", using concepts of vitalistic and existentialist philosophy, as if such a "conscience" or *self-consciousness* had been the true protagonist of the events, reacting victoriously to a Council apparently otherwise-directed by the Curia; this *artificial interpretation* forgets, among other things, that this so-called "conscience", while waiting to understand to which side the Pope was inclining, was influenced by the Episcopal Conferences and in particular by those of the "European Alliance", also endowed with remarkable financial resources.

---

[52] R. DE MATTEI, op. cit., p. 264.

4.

THE VIOLATION OF THE PRINCIPLE OF LEGALITY IN THE CONTESTED REJECTION OF THE *DE FONTIBUS REVELATIONIS* SCHEMA

The violation of the legality and the delegitimization of the Council regularly constituted according to the law (what Romano Amerio calls the "Prepared Council"), was sealed the day the schema *De Fontibus Revelationis*, the first of the famous seven mentioned above, was presented. Here there was a resounding new breach of legality and again the novators succeeded in achieving their goals thanks once again to the support of John XXIII.

The indoctrination of the bishops

It was November 14, 1962. The schema was attacked headlong by the novators with the now familiar accusations, endlessly repeated: it was not "pastoral", it was not "ecumenical", "it represented only one school of thought" (the "Roman" school, of course). A doctrinal error was even repeatedly attributed to it because it declared "two sources" of Revelation instead of "only one". Thus, the centuries-old doctrine of the Church on the sources of Revelation was now a "mistake". The Council of Trent and Vatican I, both dogmatic, which had codified and put on the same level Sacred Scripture and Tradition,[53] would, therefore, have incurred a doctrinal error!

These aberrations derived from the "teologoumena" of Karl Rahner and his companions, who, thanks to the support of their cardinal protectors, who were backed by their respective Episcopal Conferences, had been able to indoctrinate the bishops very well, in the month before the opening of the discussion.[54]

The fact that hundreds of bishops allowed themselves to be influenced by heterodox theologians, who for that matter had already

---

[53] DS, 783/1501.

[54] R.M. WILTGEN, pp. 48-49; SPADAFORA, *La "Nuova Esegesi"*, op. cit., pp. 158-159.

been officially censored by the Magisterium, under Pius XII, demonstrates the impressive decadence of broad layers of the Episcopate. The Dominican Marie-Dominique Chenu, for example, was led to the Council by Msgr. Claude Rolland, bishop of a Malagasy diocese, who, in the letter of April 1962 with which the latter elected him his theological counselor, wrote to him: "... the Council is approaching; I do not have time to prepare myself; of what will be proposed to my reflection I know nothing, apart from what the newspapers say... ".[55] And yet, Msgr. Rolland had received *almost three years before* the circular letter of Msgr. Tardini asking for his opinion on the issues to be discussed at the Council! A particularly distressful impression is provoked by the interventions in the Council that a Melchite bishop had Fr. Chenu himself prepare in French: the vindication of the great Eastern theological tradition, stated, however, in polemics with Rome, in the hands of Chenu "*sapit comicum*" because it gives birth to the (heretical) claim of the vindication of, so to speak, the socialist Christ, or the Christ "of the poor", in the manner of a Helder Câmara.[56]

A dramatic turn of events

The battle around the schema became fiercely heated, and reached a point in which the schema seemed dead, because the detractors were numerous and many of them even proposed the withdrawal of the schema. But after five congregations and a full 85 interventions for or against it (those opposed were in the majority), it was necessary to begin the examination of the individual chapters. Given the situation, the Presidency of the Council (on November 20) considered it appropriate to have the assembly vote on the question: "whether the discussion should be interrupted".

According to the regulations (art. 39 § 1), a two-thirds majority was required to approve the question, which was not reached. Out of

---

[55] M.-D. CHENU, pp. 66-67 n. 22. Msgr. Rolland was Chenu's source for what concerned the discussions in the conciliar hall. Faced with such statements, one wonders what certain bishops with a progressive slant managed to understand about the conciliar debate, and what value should actually be given to their participation in the Council.

[56] Ibid., pp. 132-134 n. 183.

2,209 voters, 1,368 requested a suspension of the debate, and 822 voted for its continuation. According to the procedure, the discussion should have continued the following day and was to continue: thus concluded, in fact, the general secretary, Msgr. Felici, concluding the session. The day after, however, on November 21st, there was *a dramatic turn of events*: a message was read in the conciliar hall according to which the Pontiff, worried about the long, laborious and uncertain discussion that was looming, had decided that the schema would be revised by a special commission; a *mixed commission*, because it was made up of members of the Theological Commission and members of the Secretariat for Christian Unity with their respective presidents: Ottaviani and Bea.[57] The mixed commissions were provided for by the regulations (art. 58 § 2), but only on the assumption that the amendments proposed by the Council Fathers "concerned several commissions". In this case, the only commission with jurisdiction was the Theological Commission while the Secretariat for Christian Unity had no jurisdiction. It was known, however, to be a progressive stronghold.

In this new (mixed) commission, the novators were certainly not in the minority.[58] But perhaps the most serious fact was that the Pope *had disavowed the application of the regulations made by the Presidency of the Council* and, moreover, again in an informal way, "*vivae vocis oraculo*".

---

[57] R.M. WILTGEN, pp. 50-51.

[58] R.M. WILTGEN, pp. 50-51; F. SPADAFORA, *La 'Nuova Esegesi'*, op. cit., p. 154. The votes in favor of interrupting the discussion were undoubtedly many. The voting took place in a heated and confused atmosphere. It seems, however, that a certain number of bishops, not very knowledgeable on the matter of assemblies and votes, made a mistake: they voted *placet*, that is, *yes* to the interruption of the discussion, convinced that they were voting in favor of the schema and thus to continue the discussion, to maintain which they should have instead voted *non-placet*, i.e., *no* to the interruption. The point was highlighted by R. DE MATTEI, op. cit., p. 262, with the source cited therein. The numbers reported by the historian are as follows: 1,368 votes in favor of suspension, 822 (or 868) against, 19 blank votes. 105 votes short of the two-thirds required by the regulations (op. cit., ibid.).

An unscrupulous operation

"Of course, with this intervention that suddenly changed the Council's decision and derogated from the regulation of the assembly", wrote Amerio, "there was a *break in legality*, moving from the collegiate regime to the monarchist regime. The result of the vote could be nullified by the Pope if a defect in legality had occurred or if a reform of the law had preceded the vote, as actually followed under Paul VI, who returned to a simple majority. But, in the terms in which it happened, the papal intervention constitutes a typical superimposition of the Pope over the Council, all the more remarkable since the Pope was presented at that time as a guardian of the Council's freedom. This overlap is not a "*motus proprius*", but is due to grievances and solicitations [of the innovators] which, treating the qualified majority [of the two-thirds] required by the Regulation as a "legal fiction", bypassed it and got the Pope to recognize the principle of the simple majority".[59] The seriousness of what had happened did not escape some observers, who at the time were even able to affirm, unfortunately without being mistaken: "It can be said that with this vote of November 20 [1962] the era of the Counter-Reformation closes and a new era opens up, unpredictable in its consequences, for Christianity".[60]

The novators rejoiced once again. In Chenu's *Diary*, under "November 21st", we read: "I am at the end of the session, in St. Peter's. The bishops are exiting lively and cheerful, for the most part. Msgr. Rolland, with a steady and luminous joy, gives me the news: the Pope has intervened [...] We're coming out of the impasse!".[61] In his *Journal of a Soul*, John XXIII praised himself for his intervention: "Apparently the good current has resumed its natural course. And all bless the Pope because he has provided for it by forming a Special Commission".[62] That "all" blessed the Pope was not true at all.[63]

---

[59] R. AMERIO, § 41 (p. 73).

[60] Phrase by P. Robert Roquette quoted by R. DE MATTEI, p. 263.

[61] M.-D. CHENU, p. 117.

[62] Ibid., p. 117 n. 143.

[63] For the confusion provoked by his decision, see the *Storia del Concilio Vaticano II*, cit., 2, V. *Il primo conflitto dottrinale*, by GIUSEPPE RUGGIERI, pp.

A proof of the unscrupulousness of the whole operation lies, in our opinion, in the fact that "L'Osservatore Romano" of November 25, 1962, in announcing the composition of the new (mixed) commission, indicated the schema to be reviewed with the term "Divine Revelation" and no longer with that of "Sources of Revelation". "The Commission has been constituted", it wrote, "for the revision of the *De Divina Revelatione* schema". The names of the cardinal composing the commission followed. Among them, five were novators: Bea, Liénart, Frings, Meyer, Joseph Lefebvre; three were faithful to dogma: Ottaviani, Ruffini, Browne.[64] We do not believe it was a slip of the tongue, even though the text appears contradictory since the "revision" by the force of things had to concern the old schema, which the progressive cardinals did not want to accept, and which was identifiable thanks to its original title, *De Fontibus Revelationis*. But obviously they did not want to wait for the beginning of the work of the "mixed" commission to change the name of the schema and make it clear which way the wind was blowing.

Naturally, there were high-level meetings in those days, well-documented today. On the evening of November 20, the day before the surprising turn of events, Cardinals Meyer, Léger and Montini went to visit John XXIII.[65] Giuseppe Alberigo writes: "The Pope's decision to validate the vote in the sense of postponing the schema to a mixed commission between the Doctrinal Commission and the Secretariat for Unity was supported by Cardinal Léger".[66] In reality, there had been no "validation" by the Pope since there was nothing to "validate". It was a legitimate vote, perfectly legal in the way it was carried out, the result of which John XXIII did not "validate" but *disregarded*, violating the conciliar legality established by himself. The (deleterious) influence attributed to the Canadian Cardinal Paul-

---

259-293; p. 292 n. 91. This author is completely silent about the illegality committed by John XXIII.

[64] R.M. WILTGEN, p. 51; M.-D. CHENU, pp. 122-123, n. 159.

[65] PH. LEVILLAIN, p. 255. See also M.-D. CHENU, pp. 122-123 and *Storia del Concilio Vaticano II*, 2, cit., pp. 290-293.

[66] G. ALBERIGO, *Concilio acefalo? L'evoluzione degli organi direttivi del Vaticano II*, in G. ALBERIGO (ed.), *Il Vaticano II fra attese e celebrazioni*, collection of essays, Il Mulino, Bologna 1995, pp. 193-238; p. 203 n. 23.

Émile Léger (an ultra-progressive element, denounced to the Holy Office by "conservative" Catholics and yet benevolently "encouraged" by Pope Roncalli)[67] cannot diminish John XXIII's responsibility: it was his duty to enforce the regulations. For that matter, it seems that he did not limit himself to *encouraging* the novators. Among other things, he imposed the Bishop of Livorno, Msgr. Emilio Guano, among the pontifically-nominated members of the mixed commission, after the Italian bishops had blatantly rejected him, on October 20, 1962.[68]

A breach of legality

When the Pope intervenes to enforce the rules of a Council, he is not superimposing himself on it, but is integrating perfectly with it, since he is exercising his function as guarantor of the legality of the Council's legal system, which he himself issues. This does not happen, however, when there is an intervention that sanctions an illegality or even brings it about, as in the case in question, and moreover "*vivae vocis oraculo*". Indeed, on closer inspection, John XXIII did not tolerate or sanction an illegality committed by others, *but committed it himself,* disregarding the result of a legitimate vote and ordering that the Council proceed in the opposite direction of that result!

Amerio notes that John XXIII's action does not conform to the (wisely constructed) image of this Pope as the guardian of the Council's freedom (against the supposed scheming of the Curia), both because of the nature of his intervention (which went against conciliar legality), and because it aimed at satisfying the subversive element, which made its pressure felt right from the start of the session and wanted to get rid of juridical forms that it considered an obstacle to its own designs. Amerio does not mention names, but among the

---

[67] "I welcomed […] Card. Léger the Archbishop of Montreal in Canada, whom I was glad to encourage amid his troubles brought to him by France and the Holy Office", entry of the *Journal of a Soul*, on October 21, 1962, quoted by the editor of *Diario* of Chenu, p. 69 n. 32. Today, Quebec, victim of the so-called "peaceful revolution" initiated by Cardinal Léger, is one of the most de-Christianized regions of the West.

[68] See CHENU's *Diario*, cit., at p. 88: "[…] but Glorieux [the theologian of Cardinal Liénart] assures me that the Holy Father is 'rescuing' him".

"grievances" and "requests" to which he refers, it is impossible not to include some statements by the controversial Cardinal Giacomo Lercaro, one of the most prominent "modernizers" in Italy at that time, which at the very least demonstrate a poor sense of the law. He stated that the procedural rules, requiring a qualified two-thirds majority, led "to the absurd consequence of making the vote of a rather narrow minority prevail over that of a strong majority". In his opinion, this constituted an "obvious weak point in the procedural rules".[69] In Fr. Chenu's diary we find a similar thought: "Thus a minority imposes deliberation [on a schema] that a strong majority rejects".[70] But it was not the minority that was imposing "deliberation" on the schema; this had been imposed, instead, by the *principle of legality* that presided over the legitimately constituted order; a fundamental principle, which requires respect for procedure: it was the command of law that imposed it, not the will of a minority.

The novators' sophisms

According to the opinion of the novators, which still today is dominant in progressive historiography, the Pope's "coup de force" could not be called illegal because "it restored the majority's rights".[71] This opinion is based on the thesis that the question proposed to the conciliar hall by Msgr. Federici ("whether the discussion should be interrupted") was improper, because it distorted the application of the principle of the qualified (two-thirds) majority established in art. 39 § 1 of the regulations. And for what reason? Because "the Fathers who were going to vote *placet* were not those favorable to the schema, but those who wished to postpone the discussion while those who were to vote *non-placet* were those who defended the schema and therefore opposed the interruption".[72] If the proposed question had been instead: "whether the discussion should continue", supposing an identical formation of the two groups, there would only have been 822 *placets* in favor of continuing, well below the two-thirds majority

---

[69] Quoted in R.M. WILTGEN, p. 50.
[70] M.-D. CHENU, p. 116.
[71] PH. LEVILLAIN, p. 167, 255.
[72] Ibid., p. 253.

foreseen by the regulations and therefore the debate would have to be suspended automatically.

We do not believe that the proposed question (after heated discussion among the ten members of the Presidency) was improper.

First of all, it should be said that illegality could not take place here, because it was one of the powers of the Council Presidency to ask the question in the manner it deemed most appropriate. Art. 4 § 2 of the regulations said that "according to the authority conferred on them by the Pope, it is the duty of the ten cardinals chosen by the Pope to direct the discussions of the Fathers and the entire discipline of the Council", a discipline which surely included how to conduct the voting. Was it then a matter of a misinterpretation of art. 39 § 1, a kind of "curial" cunning? But what did art. 39 § 1 say? "To have a majority in the Public Sessions, in the General Congregations and in the Conciliar Commissions, two-thirds of the votes of the Fathers present are required, except for the elections, in which the CIC, can. 101 § 1, 1° is applied [which provided for the criterion of the absolute majority or half plus one of the votes] and except for cases in which the Supreme Pontiff has established otherwise".[73] As we can see, the article established the criterion according to which for each vote, to be carried out in the public sessions of the Council, and in its regular sessions (or "Congregations") forbidden to the public, and in the Commissions, equally forbidden to the public, the *quorum* of two-thirds was always necessary for the approval of what was being put to a vote. This criterion was to be applied without exception, and to some, as we have seen, it seemed too rigid.

Dossetti's opinion

It is interesting to note that, in the aforementioned memorandum, which also concerned possible amendments to the Council regulations, Dossetti, Lercaro's consultant, faithful on this occasion to his training as a jurist, *demanded* that the qualified majority principle be maintained. "Point 3", he wrote, "Inflexible defense of the rule of art. 39 § 1, which establishes the need for a two-thirds qualified majority for each decision. Every so often you hear someone mention

---

[73] *Ordo*, cit., in AAS, cit., p. 624: "*Ad constituendam maioritatem in Sessionibus publicis, etc.*".

the possibility that this majority be reduced. However, it is absolutely necessary to insist that a Council, as an assembly of divine right representing the whole Church, differs in this from a democratic assembly: for it cannot be the simple majority system of democratic formalism. If the Council represents the Church, which is in Christ, the principle of the majority cannot apply to it, but that of unanimity, even if it is a non-material but moral unanimity. Moral unanimity is that which differs only by a small fraction from an absolute unanimity. Therefore one could have reasonably hoped for the guarantee of a majority even greater than two-thirds, at least for doctrinal decisions. But in any case it would not be acceptable, regarding the doctrinal decrees, to be content with a majority of less than two-thirds, currently foreseen by the regulations".[74]

In this defense, in which, despite the "conciliarist" aura that pervades it (the Council is defined as an "assembly of divine right" when it is instead a body of the Church's ecclesiastical constitution), we seem to hear an echo of something of the traditional teaching of the Church, the final point should also be noted: given the nature of the Council, a majority of less than two-thirds is ineligible for decisions concerning "doctrinal decrees". These decisions must be as close as possible to unanimity and in any case cannot be made with a majority of less than two-thirds. The importance of the topics under discussion demands this. And the discussion on *De Fontibus* concerned a doctrinal decree, that is, it concerned the dogma of the faith (and not a movement like Focolare or the Italian Catholic Youth Society).

The rule contained in art. 39 § 1 was therefore perfectly justified in the eyes of Dossetti himself, who, despite his "Catholic-communist" militancy in the shadow of Lercaro, had evidently not lost (at least judging from this memorandum) a sense for the law or the doctrinal meaning, for that matter, of a true Ecumenical Council.

A perfectly justified application

In our opinion, one must therefore consider the application of art. 39 § 1 by the Presidency of the Council to be perfectly justified, in posing the criticized question in that manner.

---

[74] Text in M.-D. CHENU, p. 103 n. 110.

In the discussion on *De Fontibus* a schema approved by the Pope, and containing the traditional teaching of the Church on this fundamental aspect of dogma, was undergoing a massive and articulated attack. Among the critics were those who wanted the outright withdrawal of the schema, as well as those who wanted to postpone the discussion to allow for a revision of the schema in the meantime. In such a situation, it was logically up to the critics of the schema to prove that they were in the majority. It was therefore necessary to verify that the will to interrupt and postpone the discussion was enough to garner two-thirds of the vote.

It would have been incorrect to ask the question the other way around (whether the discussion should continue) because, according to how the discussion was going, what was to be verified was the desire to interrupt it, not to continue it: *this* was the majority to be verified, because *this* was the majority that was emerging. According to the regulations, that majority had to prove that they had two-thirds of the votes. There was therefore no impropriety and no curial cunning. The question posed to the Assembly was perfectly in line with the letter and with the spirit of art. 39 § 1.

A further argument in favor of the decision then taken, of a more general but more pregnant nature, is the following: it was inadmissable to claim that a schema of a Dogmatic Constitution approved by the Pope required the verification of a majority in order to continue the discussion. No one could make such a claim, because that majority was to be taken for granted, it was assumed, given the nature of the Holy Church, in which the members of the hierarchy are called, by canon law and divine law, to defend the deposit of faith, keeping it uncontaminated. What had to be verified was, if anything, a majority of the opposite mind; an unheard-of event, but one which, as we know, actually took place. Therefore, from this viewpoint, too, the form in which the question was posed appears entirely correct.

"Protestantism at the gates". The Pope's duty

In the end, how should one answer the novators' thesis, according to which the Pope's intervention was justified on the practical level, because it was necessary in order to get out of the impasse, since the Council *had* to go ahead? In the following way: who said that the

Council had to continue? An ecumenical council in which, from the presentation of the first Dogmatic Constitution, approved by the Pope and concerning the Sources of Revelation, i.e., the very root of the Faith, a majority was manifesting itself that was opposed to the teaching contained therein, a majority, therefore, adverse to the doctrine always taught by the Magisterium, should have been immediately dissolved by the Pope, according to the case envisaged by can. 222 § 2 of the CIC then in force (see above). Doubtless this would have been a very serious decision, but it would have been entirely legitimate, an exercise of the *suprema potestas iurisdictionis* of the Pope (which comes to him from God) to protect the deposit of the faith which was seriously threatened. The emergence of such a heterodox majority revealed that in the Catholic Hierarchy there was a profound malaise, a metastasis that required radical interventions, the first of which could have been the resounding dissolution of the Council.

Progressive French theologians and authors have often been pleased to compare, and not wrongly, Vatican II to the French Revolution, perhaps in order to mock once more a prophecy in this sense made by Cardinal Billot in 1923, when he dissuaded Pius XI from convening an ecumenical council (the modernists always quite present among the clergy would have taken advantage of this council to launch a revolution in the Church, he said). Fr. Congar observed that the assembly of Vatican II would have effectively carried out the same (subversive) function in the Church as the General States did when convened in 1789 and which gave rise to the French Revolution. We, too, will allow ourselves a comparison with the French Revolution.

When the Third State, separated from the other two, proclaimed a National Assembly and started the revolutionary movement, "my opinion", wrote the Prince of Talleyrand, "was that the General States should be dissolved. I gave this advice to the count of Artois [the king's younger brother] who had then a certain benevolence for me [...] My advice was deemed too risky. It was an act of strength, and as for strength, there was no one around the king who knew how to use it." The copyist and collector of the prince's memoirs, Bacourt, tells us that, at the beginning of the crisis, one night indeed Talleyrand presented himself to the king's brother, who had risen to receive him, and asked him to intercede with the sovereign. The Count of Artois went to Louis XVI and spoke to him as Talleyrand desired, but returned saying that "there was nothing to do with the king, who was determined to yield rather than to cause a drop of blood to be shed".[75] According to Talleyrand, therefore, Louis XVI did not have the courage to carry out an act of force that was perfectly legal and even morally necessary since it was legitimized by the very serious violation of the Constitution of the Kingdom represented by the revolutionary action of the Third State.

We do not know if, in those fatal days of the autumn of 1962, someone ever suggested to John XXIII to dissolve the Council by his own authority. The circumstances would have made such a decision perfectly plausible. The clash in the conciliar hall had come to weigh on the very doctrinal foundation of the schema on the Sources of Revelation, since some wanted to replace the "two sources of revelation" with a single source. In other words, the Catholic doctrine that had been reaffirmed by the Council of Trent and Vatican I was to be bastardized through a formulation that would be appreciated by the heretical Protestants. In the Council, some were seeking to impose a very dangerous opinion for the dogma of the faith: the Church's doctrine was being undermined. And this under the banner of the "pastoral" and "ecumenical" approach of the Council, expressly desired by the Pope.

The phrase attributed in those days to Cardinal Ernesto Ruffini ("Protestantism is upon us") grasped perfectly the significance of the events.[76] How, in such a situation, would a Pope truly concerned about safeguarding the integrity of the deposit of faith and the salvation of souls have acted? He would have done everything possible to hinder the novators, avoiding acquiescence and

---

[75] DOMENICO BARTOLI (ed.), *Memorie di Talleyrand*, Italian trans. by D. Bartoli, Longanesi, Rome-Milan 1942, p. 50. The day after this episode, the king's brother left France, and did not return there until twenty-five years later. He would reign with the name of Charles X until the revolution of 1830.

[76] "This was Ruffini's bitter statement, after the famous session of the rejection of Ottaviani's schema [the schema on the two sources of Revelation]: 'Protestantism is at the gates" (M.-D. CHENU, p. 125, under the entry of November 28, 1962).

concessions, censoring the illegalities, reforming them, forcing compliance with the regulations. This would have led to the continuation of the discussion on the *De Fontibus* schema, chapter by chapter. If the majority had voted for changes that would overturn the schema or had voted for the withdrawal of its chapters, then the Pope, after reminding the rebels of their responsibilities, could have dissolved the Council in a perfectly legitimate way and sent everyone home.

The behavior of John XXIII

Consider, instead, what Angelo Roncalli wrote in his *Journal of a Soul* during the dramatic debate that took place in those days: "A regrettable debate about the sources of Revelation. Despite the efforts by Ottaviani's current, they're unable to contain the opposition that is proving very strong". Amazing words.[77]

The schema presented and defended by Ottaviani, and with him by the other so-called "conservatives", approved by the Pope, did not contain nor was meant to contain personal and original theses, for the simple reason that it expounded, as clearly as possible, the official and plurisecular teaching of the Magisterium. But for the Pope it was the expression of "Ottaviani's current", a partisan product! The viewpoint of a "theological current"! Did not the novators say the same?

Even more surprising words can be found in another entry: "Today, too, I listen with interest to all the voices of the Council. In large part they are critical of the proposed schemas (of Cardinal Ottaviani) which, prepared by many persons together, reveal however the somewhat arrogant fixation of a single member and the persistence of a mentality that cannot free itself from the tone of a Scholastic lesson. The semi-blindness of one eye casts a shadow on the vision of the whole. Naturally the reaction is strong, sometimes too strong... ".[78] These words cause bewilderment not only because of the play of words, done in bad taste and not without malice, about the partial blindness that had begun to afflict Cardinal Ottaviani; it is caused above all by the observation that for John XXIII the

---

[77] Text quoted in M.-D. CHENU, pp. 110-111 n. 128.
[78] Ibid., p. 115 n. 139.

exposition and defense of the dogma of the faith contained in the schema *De Fontibus* seem to be nothing but a "fixation" – and "a little arrogant" at that – "of a mentality that cannot free itself from the tone of a Scholastic lesson"; hence the reason why, "naturally", the reaction is strong. Here too, John XXIII uses the same language as the novator theologians, who, as we have seen, were contemptuous of the Magisterium: the texts of the schema, which express traditional doctrine (obviously closed to overtures towards and compromises with error) are "Scholastic" and therefore unacceptable; they are the result of the "arrogant fixation" of one member, and therefore unacceptable!

With his behavior, John XXIII essentially legitimized the interpretation that the novators gave to the "ecumenical" overtures he wanted; he legitimized, in fact, the combination "ecumenism = doctrinal change", thus allowing the Council to consolidate itself in the anomalous, revolutionary direction that the novators had wanted to give it from the beginning, in what Amerio called its "autogenic, sudden, atypical" character.[79]

The decisive event was the second break in legality, the *coup de scene* of November 21st, which sealed the process that began with the first violation of legality by Liénart on October 13, 1962. On the occasion of the first event, John XXIII sinned by omission; in the second he intervened in a manner directly opposed to conciliar legality, a fact that involved the acceptance of a very dangerous approach to the dogma of the faith. In fact, the new title imposed on the former *De Fontibus* schema, "seemed to confirm the victory of the liberal faction, which opposed the notion of two sources of revelation".[80]

The silence of the dominant historiography on these serious illegalities tolerated and committed by Pope Roncalli is explained, in our opinion, also by the insensibility of modernists and neo-modernists for the law, homologous to that which they have always shown for dogma. Thus, one of them declares in essence that he does not understand why the famous question ("whether the discussion should be interrupted") was posed in that way by Msgr. Felici.[81]

[79] R. AMERIO, § 43 (p. 76).
[80] R. M. WILTGEN, p. 51.
[81] *Storia del Concilio Vaticano II*, cap. V, vol. 2, pp. 289-290.

5.

DEI VERBUM, FRUIT OF THE "PARALLEL COUNCIL": THE POPE'S PLAN

The gradual conquest of the Theological Commission

The new schema entitled *De Divina Revelatione*, which eventually became the highly contested *Dei Verbum*, was therefore the product of the modernizing approach that the novators succeeded in imposing on the Council, thanks to the work by the Secretariat of Cardinal Bea, called by John XXIII to be part of the new "mixed" commission (see above).

Note the stages of what appears to be a strategy put in place step by step in order to control the Theological Commission which, as we said, was fundamental to controlling the work of all the commissions. As already mentioned, the "progressive" elements were present among the members and *consultores* of the Theological Commission since the preparatory phase, but in a clear minority. After the vote of October 20, 1962, held in the manner and with the results we have seen (see above), the ratio had changed in favor of the progressives, who now constituted half of the elected members. This ratio was substantially maintained even with the papal appointees, nine for each commission.[82] Now, with the establishment of the "mixed" commission, the Theological Commission was subjected to the deadly embrace of Bea's Secretariat. A few more moves (authored by Paul VI) and the coveted definitive control would be achieved.

---

[82] The limited impact on the balance of the commissions by the nine members (out of twenty-five) named by the Pope is documented with a careful analysis by PH. LEVILLAIN, pp. 224-230.

The "canons" of the "parallel Council", that is, of false ecumenism

The novators' strategy succeeded in burying what Amerio called "the prepared council", prepared by the legitimate Commissions, according to the orthodox doctrinal approach guaranteed by the Roman Curia. Of the twenty schemas of constitutions developed in the preparatory phase, only the one on the Liturgy was saved, because it was the only one acceptable to the neo-modernists. The three-year work, approved by John XXIII, was discarded without the latter batting an eyelid. But the *new* Council that replaced the "prepared Council" was only partly "autogenic and sudden". In reality, it represented a further and ruinous development of the "parallel Council" (as we like to call it) that had been articulated since the preliminary phase of the works, with the encouragement of Pope Roncalli. This "parallel" Council developed the ecumenical direction in the "pastoral" way desired by Roncalli, a way that had not found expression in the schemas elaborated under the control of the Theological Commission, with the (partial) exception of the schema on the Liturgy.

The *ecumenically correct* language, that is, not the Scholastic but the so called ecumenical one, that the final schemas and texts had to manifest without exception, was based on the following *canons*, derived from the directives given by John XXIII starting from the announcement of the Council (January 25, 1959) until the opening speech of the same (the Allocution *Gaudet Mater Ecclesia*) of October 11, 1962, summarizing those canons in a kind of "summa":[83]

1. no dogmatic definition; 2. no condemnation of errors (instead of using charity & mercy to the errant individual so that he might convert, [already by the simple fact of not condemning them] charity and mercy were in fact used towards the errors. Condemnation was thus replaced by an outright abdication of the Pope's duty as the Vicar of Christ on earth); 3. an enunciation of the truths of faith "through the forms of inquiry and the literary formulation of modern thought", as the vulgate text (Italian and French) of the Allocution stated; in any

---

[83] Remember, for example, the clear declaration, not open to alternate interpretations, that the Council would not condemn any error, made at the general audience on November 16, 1960 (PH. LEVILLAIN, p. 57 note n. 1).

case the truths were to be enunciated in a "pastoral" way, that is, a way acceptable to Protestants and the Orthodox (a classical example is the use in the Council's text of the ambiguous Protestant concept of the "history of salvation"), a directive that involved *silence* about essential truths of faith, as in the case of the dogma of transubstantiation and the expiatory and propitiatory character of the Eucharistic Sacrifice, or near silence (as in the case of the dogma of original sin, mentioned by the Council only in passing and in a very ambiguous way) and the adoption of a generic language, constructed using a large number of passages of the Holy Scriptures, the Fathers and ancient liturgical books in such a way as to allow a generic interpretation of the truths contained in them, and therefore acceptable also for non-Catholics; 4. the "*aggiornamento*" (updating) of Catholicism to purely worldly, "secular", and largely political values, such as peace in the world (an *idée fixe* of John XXIII), universal brotherhood, progress, democracy, the dignity of man, freedom of religion based on the beliefs of individual conscience, in order to "purify them"; 5. the recognition of the *equal dignity* not only of the heretical and schismatic sects but also of the other religions, unrevealed, and therefore invented by men; 6. the pursuit of unity *with the "separated brothers"* (without their repentance and return to the Church) and of the *human race* (without its conversion to Christ) through "dialogue" (hence the imperative to discover in "dialogue" what the whole non-Christian and non-Catholic world can share with Catholics, in order to build a common vision of the world's contingent problems, beginning with that of peace – in short, instead of missionary activity to convert those who strayed, a confident and optimistic "dialogue" with error, and "listening" to what the world can teach the Catholic Church!).

John XXIII, the enigma

The Council prepared under the direction of Ottaviani and Tromp did not and could not answer to such criteria.

Had not John XXIII repeatedly affirmed, even in the opening speech of the Council, that the deposit of faith had to be kept intact? As was their duty, Ottaviani and Tromp had worked in this direction, ignoring as far as possible the Pope's continuous references to the fact that the deposit had to be maintained but "according to the needs of the times" or "studied and exhibited" according to these needs, as he said in the Latin version of the inaugural address, and in the context of a Magisterium with a particularly "pastoral" slant. Thus the schema of the Dogmatic Constitution *De deposito fidei pure custodiendo*, after having clearly exposed the traditional doctrine of the Church, condemned an impressive series of errors: agnosticism, existentialism, atheistic materialism, materialistic and pantheistic evolutionism, doctrinal relativism, neopelagianism and naturalism or false humanism, spiritualism and reincarnation, etc.[84] There was a need for these solemn condemnations. This is demonstrated in retrospect, not only by the frightening corruption of morals now afflicting the West in its entirety, but also by the current spread of agnosticism, doctrinal relativism, false humanism, spiritualism and the doctrine of reincarnation among Catholics themselves. These are some of the false doctrines with which "dialogue" has contaminated the healthy faith of the past. And the severe hostility of the novators to the aforementioned schema is also better understood in retrospect.[85]

John XXIII wanted, therefore, to keep the deposit of faith intact and at the same time to avoid the condemnation of errors. Not only that: he wanted the doctrine to be expounded to be clothed with the forms of modern thought, with a "predominantly pastoral" Magisterium, which in this way came to be the ad hoc form of exercising of the Magisterium, against the whole Tradition of the Church. Did he not realize that he wanted things that were contradictory and to re-propose that separation between the substance of the doctrine and its formulation already condemned by the Magisterium?[86] What, then, was his true thought?

Allowing the facts to speak

It seems to us that the Pope's true intentions appear unequivocally from certain qualifying facts.

---

[84] PH. LOVEY, p. 130.

[85] M.-D. CHENU, p. 57 n. 64.

[86] On the incongruity of John XXIII's "abstaining" from his duties as Pope, cf. R. AMERIO, § 40 (p. 69 ff).

We have already mentioned how, in the preliminary phase of the Council, John XXIII had introduced as consultants to the Theological Commission a number of theologians in the odor of heresy as well as some already censored by the Holy Office. He reiterated that the Council should keep the deposit of faith intact. But was that the way to implement such a goal, by inserting within the Theological Commission individuals whose works were notoriously filled with false doctrines, both old and new? Theologians, moreover, who had never repented of their mistakes and who had locked themselves in a protracted silence while at the same time acting as victims of the Curia? And what about the faculty granted to the Council Fathers in art. 33 § 1 of the regulations he promulgated, to be able to reject any prepared schema – a faculty, thus, which was openly in contradiction, as we have seen, with the Pope's power of jurisdiction and the Church constitution?

Another qualifying fact is the endorsement Roncalli gave in the end to the schema on the Liturgy, of which in the preparatory phase he was not entirely convinced on some points. This schema was harshly attacked in the conciliar hall by Ottaviani, Parente, Browne, Traglia and even "demolished in twelve places" by Msgr. Dante, secretary of the Sacred Congregation of Rites, and Msgr. Vagnozzi, also an eminent liturgist. Despite the obvious and well-founded opposition of extremely competent figures on the subject, John XXIII evidently did not have the courage to oppose the novators.[87]

Moreover, despite having approved the dogmatic schemas elaborated by the Theological Commission, John XXIII not only tolerated but even encouraged the action of the novators, who were contesting dogma and intended to destroy those same schemas. In our view, we have a proof of such encouragement in the so-called "Suenens plan".

In March 1962, this Belgian cardinal, a member of the Central Preparatory Commission, complained to the Pope of the overly

---

[87] On this point cf. R. DE MATTEI, pp. 238-254, which reproduces extensive excerpts from the interventions, as well as Ph. Levillain, pp. 161-162. By criticizing a schema approved by the Pope, Ottaviani was not contradicting himself: the schema was not that of a Dogmatic Constitution and he was not asking for its withdrawal but for its revision. See also PH. LEVILLAIN, pp. 161-162 and R.M. WILTGEN, pp. 140-141.

"conservative" character of the elaborate schemas and of their excessive number. John XXIII asked him to send him a project of his. Suenens gave him a preliminary note, which indicated how the "pastorality" of the Council should be understood; this note was approved orally by the Pope. Subsequently (late April 1962) Suenens transformed it into a project (the "Suenens plan"), made known to Montini and Léger, among others. John XXIII then ordered Cardinal Cicognani, Secretary of State, to send photocopies of the project to several cardinals, to make them aware of it. He then commissioned Suenens to meet Döpfner, Montini, Siri (the only "conservative"), Liénart, Lercaro, to create a group document, subsequently presented in the conciliar hall by Suenens on December 4, 1962. This document seems to have left a trace in the papal message of December 12, 1962.[88]

According to this entirely reliable reconstruction of the facts, we see here Pope Roncalli even guiding the ranks of protest, so as to direct them to a specific and concrete result.

John XXIII was always careful to reiterate what he considered his true thought, to avoid misunderstandings as to what was meant by the "*aggiornamento*" of the Church. Faced with interpretations such as that of Cardinal Siri, which saw in his opening speech of the Council principally the defense of doctrine and tradition, he, in his speech for the new year held as usual at the College of Cardinals (January 1963), citing himself in the vernacular version, which was more audacious in some points than the Latin one, especially in the famous phrase in which he affirmed that doctrine must be "studied and expounded through the forms of inquiry and the literary formulation of modern thought", made it clear that the opening speech was valid above all in the novelties that it enunciated.[89]

Likewise, in the *Ordo* or regulations issued on December 6, 1962, on the eve of the scheduled suspension of the Council for a pause or intersession, and containing the establishment of a new body, the *Coordination Commission*, composed of cardinals appointed by him, as well as the directives to be observed for the continuation of the work

---

[88] PH. LOVEY, p. 138.

[89] The note is from prof. Alberto Melloni, editor of Chenu's *Diario*, p. 101 n. 109.

during the intersession or pause period, John XXIII "insisted on the necessity that the purpose of the Council [enunciated in the central passages of the abovementioned *Gaudet Mater Ecclesia*, which were reproduced word for word] should guide all its work".[90]

Speeches are facts, even if they are made up of words. Another essential fact in John XXIII's behavior was his openness to *collegiality*. Initially, he tolerated the heterodox initiative of those Episcopal Conferences which, as we have seen, aimed at rewriting the schemas approved by the Pope. He then allowed them to participate actively in the handling of the October 20, 1962 elections. From a de facto tolerance of their increasingly substantive intrusiveness, John XXIII then passed to an open consecration of their role in the Council. This is shown from the *Ordo* of December 6, mentioned above. It codified a series of the novators' demands because, among other things, it gave space to the "special and mixed sub-commissions", which had to make their contribution to the selection and revision of the schemas, under the direction of the Coordination Commission. The revised schemas, after the "generic" papal approval (*generice facta*), had to be transmitted to the bishops, preferably through the presidents of the Episcopal Conferences.[91]

The preliminary pontifical approval, revisited

Regarding this "generice facta" approval, Alberigo takes the opportunity to reiterate the thesis of progressive historiography, that the Pope's approval of the preparatory schemas did not refer to their content: "So, [it was] a consent to send [the schemas] and not an approval of their merits, thus disregarding the widespread argument that discussing and – above all – rejecting the preparatory schemas would have implied less devotion to the Pope who had approved them". But a careful examination of the text of the *ordo* in question

---

[90] G. ALBERIGO, *Dinamiche e procedure nel Vaticano II. Verso la revisione del Regolamento del Concilio (1962-1963)*, in *Cristianesimo e Storia* 13 (1992) pp. 115-164; p. 124.

[91] Alberigo highlights the similarities between the entire *ordo*, signed by the Secretary of State, and a proposal elaborated by Fr. Dossetti, at the request of Cardinal Döpfner (see last quoted work, pp. 122-123).

demonstrates once again, in our opinion, the inaccuracy of this interpretation.[92]

In fact, the regulation states that "the individual schemas, after having been reviewed [*recognita*] in this way [indicated in detail in the text itself] and after having obtained the general approval of the Venerable Pontiff, are to be sent to the bishops, etc.". From the grammatical, syntactic, and semantic structure of the passage, it emerges that the schemas were to be sent after they were reviewed and after being approved by Pope "*generice*". This adverb, "generically" or "in general", cannot refer to the sending of the schemas, but only to their approval. This is shown beyond the shadow of a doubt by the syntax. It is therefore a papal approval given to the reviewed text (*recognitum*). Moreover, it cannot refer to the sending of the schemas, because this sending, like that of any document, is a specific administrative act and therefore it makes no sense to state that it is the object of a "generic approval" or "approval in general". The approval concerning the sending will instead always be specific, it will be qualified as the approval for sending, explicitly declared. A general or generic approval can be given to a text and cannot concern anything other than its content, its merits.[93]

What will the adverb "generically" mean in our case? To us the meaning seems obvious: that we are not faced with a *specific*, definitive and irrevocable approval, which would have cut off any possible debate on the schemas, but with an approval "in general" on the merits of the texts in question read by the Pope; that is, including an implicit declaration of their doctrinal orthodoxy in all their parts (see above). This kind of declaration was indispensable both according to the ecclesiastical constitution and according to the divine constitution of the Church, since it allowed all those who wanted to discuss and vote on the texts to be sure of two things: 1) that the texts did not contain mere personal opinions of their authors; 2) that they were in conformity with the deposit of faith in all their parts (if, then, they

---

[92] G. ALBERIGO, *Concilio acefalo?*, op. cit., pp. 205-206.

[93] AS, I/1, p. 98. This is the original text: "*Singula schemata postquam hoc modo recognita fuerint, atque Augusti Pontificis approbationem generice factam obtinuerint, ad Episcopos mittentur…*".

proved not to be so, totally or partially, it would have been the Pope's responsibility).

Having closed this parenthesis, we once more take up the thread of the discourse on John XXIII's true plan.

Divestiture of the Pope in favor of collegiality

On the level of principles, John XXIII's weighing more heavily in favor of the principle of collegiality is even more evident in the apostolic letter *Mirabilis ille*, addressed to the individual bishops on January 6, 1963 to continue to work on the themes of the Council during the intersession.

Pope Roncalli wrote: "It is natural that the Ecumenical Council receive its general norms from the Roman Pontiff, who has summoned it; but at the same time it is up to the Bishops to establish, in observance of those norms, the mode (*modum statuere*) in which it will take place with due liberty". It will be necessary, continued the letter, for the Pope to approve all the decrees of the Council so that they have the force of law; nevertheless, "it is the duty of the Council Fathers to propose these sacred decrees, to discuss them, to write them down in due form and eventually to sign them together with the Roman Pontiff".[94] As Levillain also notes, these reflections of John XXIII "contained in germ the notion of co-responsibility included in the principle of collegiality, which *Lumen Gentium* would later establish".[95] But the "co-responsibility" actually expressed a downgrading by the Pope of his own authority, since he discredited his own "*approbatio*" (and in a matter of such great import), reducing it to an almost notarial act, and conceived himself as a simple guardian of the formal correctness of the bishops' free initiative.

The oblique strategy of John XXIII

The actions and declarations of John XXIII show, therefore, how he encouraged and supported the component of the "parallel Council" represented by the subversive action of bishops organized in study groups and pressure groups (with a large contribution of

---

[94] *Ordo* etc., in AAS, LV (1963), cit., p. 152.
[95] PH. LEVILLAIN, pp. 272-273.

theologians in the odor of heresy) and above all organized in the Episcopal Conferences, in which the schema of the constitution on the liturgy (*Sacrosanctum Concilium*) already recognized an uncommon and vast competence in liturgical matters, although Msgr. Dante had underlined the serious deviation from the Tradition of the Church represented by the recognition of this competence.[96]

From all this it must be concluded that the support for the illegal and revolutionary action of the novators corresponded to the true thought of John XXIII, while his approval of the schemas developed under the effective doctrinal control of the Theological Commission of Ottaviani and Tromp was evidently for him only an act of duty that he could not avoid because of his office. Indeed, we must ask: since the approved schemas (except that on the Liturgy) did not reflect the "pastoral" and "ecumenical" approach of the Council expressly desired by him, why had John XXIII approved them? In particular, why had he not openly refused to give his assent to the schemas of the Dogmatic Constitutions? In reality, he could not objectively refuse to do so: he had to ratify the merits of those schemas, since they reaffirmed the traditional doctrine of the Church, what the Magisterium had always taught over the centuries. The scandal would have been enormous if he had returned them to their sender! It was thus necessary to fall back on an *oblique strategy*, one of circumvention, and even resort to a *war of attrition*.

The "delegitimization" of the Council and the Papacy

This strategy, simultaneously aimed at penetrating and circumventing, was articulated on several different levels. On the one hand, it allowed, as we have seen, the unlawful pressure that certain forces exercised on the Commissions and on the Council from the outside, favoring their illegitimate and gradual insertion in the Council in the name of collegiality. On the other hand, it initiated a reform of the regulations – which would be completed by Paul VI – whose first act was the establishment of the aforementioned Coordination Committee. The purpose of this reform consisted above all in

---

[96] R.M. WILTGEN, p. 28.

establishing governing bodies of the Council that would guide it in the direction willed by John XXIII.

In his essay on the evolution of the governing bodies of Vatican II, Alberigo highlights the "evolution" of these bodies. He moves from the observation that "the plethoric Council of Presidency" had proved incapable of guaranteeing the Council the necessary guidance. Moreover, "after the decision of November 19 [in reality November 20] to continue the debate on the *De Fontibus Revelationis* schema was disregarded by John XXIII, the Presidency appeared to be delegitimized".[97] Therefore, according to Alberigo, the Pope's gesture, the illegality of which he passes over in silence, "delegitimized" the Presidency. But can an illegal action "delegitimize" the body that is its victim? It can. But only in terms of the balance of power, certainly not in terms of law. As already mentioned, the true "delegitimization" was suffered by the Council and the Papacy, on the level of morals and prestige and, on closer inspection, also of legality.

Using the concept in the sense Alberigo intends, it seems to us that the decision of November 20 "delegitimized" the Presidency especially in the eyes of Angelo Roncalli, who did not find in it a body capable of leading the Council according to his directives. And why, didn't he find it to be such? Perhaps because of weak regulations, which gave the ten cardinals who made up the Presidency management powers as broad as they were vague? In reality it was not a problem of regulations. The Presidency appeared "delegitimized" because in it the novators and those faithful to Tradition were equally strong, with now one party, now the other prevailing. In the case of the famous question proposed regarding the interruption of the debate on the *De Fontibus* schema, the thesis (which was also quite correct, as we have seen) of the "conservative" cardinal Ruffini had been imposed against that of the novator, Cardinal Frings.[98] This means that the *thesis less pleasing to Pope Roncalli had prevailed*. This is the truth. And John XXIII's reaction was swift. He "delegitimized" the Presidency in the eyes of third parties, with no concern for the principle of legality.

---

[97] G. ALBERIGO, *Concilio acefalo?*, op. cit., pp. 193-195.
[98] PH. LEVILLAIN, pp. 252-253.

The secret rescript

This "delegitimization" had actually started even earlier. In the days of October 15-17, which were the days immediately following the *coup de main* of Cardinal Liénart, with a rescript kept secret (and found many years later by the scholars among the papers of Cardinal Siri), John XXIII had extended the responsibilities of the *Secretariatus de Concilii negotiis extra ordinem* (Secretariat for Extraordinary Affairs), established by art. 7 § 2 of the conciliar regulations, composed of seven cardinals appointed by the Pope under the Presidency of the Secretary of State, Cardinal Cicognani, and charged with "weighing new proposals [*novas peculiares quaestiones*] advanced by the Fathers and, if necessary, submitting them to the Pope".[99] These new, broader responsibilities established that the Secretariat "should follow the Council so as to grasp the points" that could or should be developed and completed. Secondly, the Secretariat itself was competent to examine the admissibility of proposals "outside of the schemas"; this implied the possibility of bypassing the alleged monopoly of the preparatory schemas, as those would have been the only ones which had obtained the assent of the Pope to be submitted to the Council. Finally, the Secretariat was to "give suggestions and advice on issues or schemas that were difficult to resolve". In essence "the Secretariat received authority over the rough and problematic aspects of the life of the conciliar assembly. The Council of Presidency remained solely responsible for regulating the progress of the General Congregations".[100] As a consequence of this, it was the Secretariat's job to guide "organically" the conciliar work until the end of the first session.[101]

The "new spirit". The responsibility of John XXIII

It is to be noted that, with this – secret – extension of powers, John XXIII de facto divested the Presidency of the Council of its

[99] For the analysis of the role played by the Secretariat in extraordinary issues, we have based our work on G. ALBERIGO, *Concilio acefalo?*, pp. 195-203.

[100] G. ALBERIGO, Ibid., pp. 197-198.

[101] Ibid., p. 202.

power well before the crisis of November 20, when he rejected the decision (imposed by the regulations) to continue the debate on *De Fontibus Revelationis*. In practice, he had been divesting it since almost the beginning of the works, which began on October 13th. He divested it after Lienart's coup involving the postponement of the Commissions elections, a coup de main he had permitted.

For the proper functioning of the work of the Assembly, it was grave not to have made public the enlargement of the responsibilities of the Secretariat for Extraordinary Affairs. Subsequently, as we have seen, John XXIII instituted the *Coordination Commission* on December 6, 1962, "with the task of coordinating and following the work of the Commissions, ensuring the conformity of the schemas with the purpose of the Council. The Commission would be presided over by the Secretary of State as the Pope's representative" and its member cardinals would be designated by the Pope.[102] In the composition of the two bodies, the Secretariat and the Commission, novators and "conservatives" appeared to be numerically equivalent, except for the greater capacity for cohesion and the greater striking force almost always demonstrated by the novators.

But the numerical balance mattered only to a certain extent. What mattered was the fact, now evident, that Angelo Roncalli sided with the novators. Everyone had noticed. The regulations of December 6, 1962 left no doubt about it. It definitively sanctioned the revolutionary movement initiated illegally by Cardinal Liénart on October 13, accepting its fundamental demands.

Let us read Chenu's diary. "Thursday, December 6th. Communiqué by the Secretary of State on behalf of the Pope. A categorical document, conceived in view of the intersession. The Fathers were satisfied. Ratification of the orientation of the Council – cf. text in my dossier [it was the novators' "orientation"]. At La Salette [at the house of the Missionaries of La Salette], during the meal, [there were] a dozen French bishops. Euphoria. Even those we know to be more *conservative* were seized by the new spirit".[103] The "new spirit" had begun to appear in the conciliar hall with John XXIII's unexpected endorsement of Cardinal Liénart and with the

---

[102] G. ALBERIGO, *Dinamiche e procedure*, cit., p. 124.
[103] M.-D. CHENU, p. 137. The italics are from the original.

consequent success of the novators in the elections of the Conciliar Commissions. In fact, some presidents of the Commissions themselves, "realized with amazement that members, who had taken an active part in the elaboration of the schemas, now were attacking them with passion".[104]

In the end, the "new spirit" began to find followers even among the bishops of the "conservative" nucleus, still substantial in number, when even the blind could see that Pope Roncalli was in fact turning out to be a "follower" of that spirit. Then that nucleus began to fall apart as the ranks of those who *ran to the aid of the victor* suddenly swelled.

---

[104] PH. LEVILLAIN, pp. 228-229.

6.

DEI VERBUM, THE FRUIT OF THE "PARALLEL COUNCIL": THE INSIDIOUS ACTION OF CARDINAL AUGUSTIN BEA'S SECRETARIAT

The éminence grise of the Council

After the two aspects of John XXIII's strategy already highlighted, it is necessary to mention a third, in order to complete the picture, concerning the Secretariat of Cardinal Augustin Bea, the true grey eminence of the Council.

In the preparatory phase, discussing art. 7 of the schema of the Dogmatic Constitution *De Ecclesia*, prepared by the Theological Commission, which proclaimed (according to dogma) the Catholic Church the *only* Church of Christ and *therefore* the only Ark of Salvation, Cardinal Augustin Bea S.J., who (obviously) did not like the article as it was not very "ecumenical", affirmed that his Secretariat (established "to promote unity among Christians") had treated the same questions "numerous times" and "with great care" and asked the Theological Commission "to constitute (together) a mixed commission, which was always rejected". He added that he had also sent to the aforementioned Commission a schema, of which there was "some trace" in *De Ecclesia*, even if "unfortunately", the Cardinal complained, "numerous points were not taken into consideration".[105]

Cardinal Bea was the head of an apparently *technical* body such as a simple Secretariat, whose institutional task (ex art. 9 of the motu proprio *Superno Dei nutu*) consisted officially of ensuring that "separated" Christians could "follow the work of the Council and more easily find the way to fulfill that unity that 'Jesus Christ asked the Father for with ardent prayers'".[106] Why, then, did he allow himself to criticize the text of a Dogmatic Constitution in the name of the Secretariat? And not only that. He also told, with an accusatory tone,

---

[105] PH. LOVEY, p. 122. We have retranslated from the translation into French. The discussions occurred in Latin.

[106] AAS, LII (1960), p. 436.

of a refusal of the Theological Commission to form a mixed commission, complaining that his suggestions had not been accepted. With what authority? In reality, Cardinal Bea spoke with the authority of one who had received from John XXIII a much wider mandate than that formally conferred upon him as president of a simple Secretariat, a body in charge of a mainly administrative function and which did not have the rank of a conciliar commission.

The "ecumenical" openness of John XXIII

To understand the oddity of this situation, one must bear in mind the origin of the body for which Cardinal Bea was responsible.

The first attempts at dialogue with the Protestant *Ecumenical Council of the Churches* had been made, starting in 1946, by the Dominican Christophe-Jean Dumont and his confrère Yves Congar. The two friars had sent a document to the Secretariat of State of Pius XII, specifically to the then Msgr. Montini.[107] Then came the establishment of the Catholic Conference for Ecumenical Questions, founded by the then Msgr. Willebrands.[108] It was not possible, however, under Pius XII, to have a "Roman office in charge of ecumenism", that is, a true Pontifical Commission for ecumenism, requested above all by Dutch and German circles and proposed in vain to Cardinal Ottaviani with the mediation of Msgr. Charrière, bishop of Geneva, Lausanne and Fribourg.[109] The Holy Office claimed for itself control of every "ecumenical" initiative, rightly afraid of negative repercussions on doctrine (which later occurred exactly as feared).

---

[107] All the data presented here on the origins of Cardinal Bea's Secretariat are taken from MAURO VELATI, *"Un indirizzo a Roma"*. *La nascita del Segretariato per l'unità dei Cristiani (1959-1960)*, in *Il Vaticano II fra attese e celebrazioni*, cit., pp. 75-118; p. 81. For a detailed analysis of its activity, see by same author *La proposta ecumenica del Segretariato per l'unità dei Cristiani*, in G. ALBERIGO – A. MELLONI (ed.), *Verso il Vaticano II (1960-1962). Passaggi e problemi della preparazione conciliare*, Genova 1993, pp. 397-343. See also *Storia del Concilio Vaticano II*, vol. 1, III, *La lotta per il concilio durante la preparazione*, by J. KOMONCHAK, pp. 177-379; p. 263 ff.

[108] M. VELATI, *"Un indirizzo a Roma"*, p. 82 ff.

[109] Ibid.

Things changed radically with John XXIII, and already in the preconciliar *vota* the German episcopal conference expressed itself collectively in favor of the establishment of a Pontifical Commission "*ad unitatem Christianorum promovendam*".[110]

Faced with the "ecumenical" openness of the new Pope, the Lateran University sent a long opinion on the problem of the union of Christians, drawn up by Prof. Giuseppe D'Ercole, who taught canon law there. It reflected the traditional approach of the Church, reiterated by Pius XI in 1928 with the Encyclical *Mortalium animos*, which the liberals had characterized as "unionist"; where "unionist" (a term they used with a derogatory sense) is the opposite of "ecumenical", expressing the concept of the return of repentant heretics and schismatics into the union with the true Church of Christ, the Catholic Church.[111] The Lateran document, in fact, proposed the establishment of a Sacred Congregation "*de Christianis ad unum gregem Christi revocandis*", charged with promoting "an apostolic and scientific missionary movement for the return to the Church of separated Christians and moral, cultural, social, religious assistance for those who return".[112] But this meant, Velati writes, that "John XXIII's directions on the ecumenical significance of the Council were not being ignored, but altered". It could not have been otherwise, we add, as these directions cannot be integrated with the Church's traditional teaching.[113]

The alternative "pole" to the Holy Office

Indeed, "the return of separated Christians to the Church" was not what John XXIII wanted. The initiative he approved of came from Germany between the end of 1959 and the beginning of 1960, through the joint action of Lorenz Jäger, bishop of Paderborn, and of the then Msgr. Augustin Bea S.J.

In March 1960, Msgr. Bea, who was made cardinal at that time, sent the Pope the proposal (formally a "plea") to create "a central

---

[110] Ibid., p. 87. Explicit proposals in this direction also came from the Catholic universities of Münster, Trier and Fribourg in Switzerland.

[111] Ibid., p. 88.

[112] Ibid., p. 89.

[113] Ibid., pp. 102-103.

body" in charge of ecumenical relations: a *"Commissio pro motione oecumenica"*. The official term used in the proposal (in order not to arouse the suspicions of the Holy Office) was *"pontificia Commissio pro unitate Christianorum promovenda"*.[114] "Bea's initial idea", Velati writes, "took its inspiration from the model of the various curial Commissions that had been set up during the last century to respond to the most diverse pastoral needs". These were commissions with a cardinal as president, appointed by the Pope, and a secretary, members and consultants.[115] The body was to coordinate the ecumenical activities, which had multiplied in the Catholic world after the announcement of the Council, "possibly working on their own initiative" with the Sacred Congregations competent in the relevant subjects.[116] In this way, Bea withdrew responsibility for ecumenism from the Holy Office.[117]

Pope Roncalli made a significant change to the project: in the private hearing of March 13, 1960, in which he appointed Bea as president of the new commission, he informed him that he wanted to "insert the new organism within the framework of the Council's preparation structure".[118] This led to the substantial exclusion of the Curia because "in the foreground were the residential bishops called to bring the contribution of pastoral experience in countries of inter-confessional coexistence".[119] In fact, they constituted six of the ten members of the Commission for Ecumenism.[120]

---

[114] Ibid., pp. 103-104.

[115] Ibid.

[116] Ibid., p. 105.

[117] Ibid.

[118] Ibid., p. 106.

[119] Ibid.

[120] For the detailed composition of the Commission, see M. VELATI, *La proposta ecumenica del Segretariato per l'unità dei Cristiani*, op. cit., p. 276 ff. Members and consultants represented almost all the cream of Catholic ecumenism *"à la nouvelle théologie"*.

"Bea's ambitious project". The root of the conflicts and the beginning of the doctrinal deviations

The *variant* desired by John XXIII was obviously reflected in the composition of the Statute submitted by Bea to the Pope himself on March 23, 1960 and contributed in an essential way to what Velati calls "Bea's ambitious project". The *Pontificium Consilium Christianorum unitati promovendae* (this was the name of the organ proposed in the statute) was to study and gathering information on the ecumenical movement, to have at its disposal a library, magazines and the like, and to direct, without centralizing, "the major centers of ecumenical activity".[121] However, and much more important, "the other curial offices [...] had to refer to the *Consilium* for every question concerning the problem of Christian unity".[122] In this way, notes the Author, "the traditional centrality of the Holy Office was relativized by creating a sort of alternative pole [...] This is the root of many successive conflicts between Bea and the leaders of the Supreme Congregation: Ottaviani did not intend to fully accept this supervisory role of the Secretariat".[123]

All the more so, we add, since from the beginning the Secretariat presented itself under the banner of *doctrinal deviation*. In fact, in a letter attached to the draft statute, and therefore certainly known to Pope Roncalli, Cardinal Bea already outlined the new "theology of baptism" which was subsequently made the basis of ecumenism. Following this "new theology", from baptism alone – which, even when it is valid, is not fruitful because, "not having the true faith, they cannot receive sanctifying grace but only the character [of baptism], which will make grace live if they abjure their heresies"[124] – Cardinal Bea drew the erroneous conclusion that it was no longer necessary *to convert and bring*

---

[121] M. VELATI, *"Un indirizzo a Roma"*, op. cit., p. 108.

[122] Ibid., p. 106.

[123] Ibid.

[124] MSGR. MARCEL LEFEBVRE, *Itinerario spirituale*, ed. it., Albano Laziale (Roma), 2000, p. 76. The thesis presented here by Msgr. Lefebvre is not his personal opinion, but corresponds to the doctrine always taught by the Church.

back (reformed and repentant) heretics to the one Church of Christ, the Catholic Church.[125]

As Romano Amerio stressed, *the Cardinal altered the Church's doctrine.* "He declared that the movement is not one of the return of the separated brethren to the Church of Rome and, following the common opinion, asserted that the Protestants are not detached completely because they have the character of baptism. However, quoting from *Mystici Corporis* of Pius XII, which reaffirms that "they are ordered to the mystical body", he came to assert that *they belong to it* and that therefore they find themselves in a situation of salvation not unlike that of Catholics (OR, 27 April 1962). He sees this union as a simple clarification of a unity already virtually present, unity of which we need only to become conscious. This unity is only virtual even in the Catholic Church, which must become aware not of itself, but of that deeper reality of the total Christ which is the synthesis of the scattered members of Christendom. Not therefore a *reversion* of one to the other, but the *conversion* of all to the center which is the profound Christ".[126]

This belonging of the heretics to the Church is, however, explicitly denied in *Mystici Corporis*. In fact, Pius XII wrote: "As you know, Venerable Brethren, from the very beginning of Our Pontificate, We have committed to the protection and guidance of heaven those who do not belong to the visible Body of the Catholic Church, etc. [...] We ask each and every one of them [the heretics] to correspond to the interior movements of grace, and to seek to withdraw from that state in which they cannot be sure of their salvation. For even though by an unconscious desire and longing they have a certain relationship with the Mystical Body of the Redeemer, they still remain deprived of those many heavenly gifts and helps which can only be enjoyed in the

---

[125] For the specific contribution of Cardinal Bea to this (new) "theology of baptism", cf. M. VELATI, *"Un indirizzo a Roma"*, p. 107, with the sources reported therein. Bea's thesis was in contradiction with what was taught by Pius XI in the Encyclical *Mortalium animos*, dated 1928, which very clearly condemned "pan-Christianism", i.e., syncretistic ecumenism, a precursor of that which later penetrated the texts of Vatican II.

[126] R. AMERIO, § 246 (p. 466). The italics come from the original text.

Catholic Church. Therefore let them re-enter Catholicism etc.".[127] And already Gregory XVI in *Mirari Vos* had pointed out that: "Wrongly [...] some of those who are not united with the Chair of Peter flatter themselves in thinking they are okay by saying they are also regenerated in the waters of salvation". In fact, the Church's constant doctrine, already expressed in the Athanasian Symbol, is that "whoever wants to save himself must first possess the Catholic faith". This doctrine, constantly proposed by the infallible Magisterium of the Church, was now casually disregarded by Cardinal Bea, who proposed one in the odor of heresy.

Bea's Secretariat, the counterpart at the Council to the Theological Commission

The external relations of the *Consilium* were initially limited to the Protestants, but later they would also be extended to the Orthodox.[128] Its task was also to send Catholic "observers" to the meetings of non-Catholics and to open negotiations for the acceptance of non-Catholic observers at the Council.[129] Moreover, "from the very beginning in Bea's mind [who thus implemented the express directive of Pope Roncalli] the new body was supposed to play an active role also in the elaboration of the schemas for the Council and not to be limited to serving as a point of contact or information for non-Catholics".[130]

From this picture the *Consilium* to be established was conceived as a sort of control or supervisory body both towards fundamental institutions of the Curia and towards the conciliar Commissions. But what was it supposed to control? The adherence of their initiatives to the direction desired by John XXIII, that is to the canons of the *new ecumenical teaching.*

---

[127] *Mystici Corporis*, English trans. from http://w2.vatican.va/content/pius-xii/en/encyclicals/documents/hf_p-xii_enc_29061943_mystici-corporis-christi.html, n. 103.

[128] M. VELATI, *"Un indirizzo a Roma"*, op. cit., p. 104.

[129] Ibid., pp. 113-114.

[130] Ibid., pp. 111-112, which records in a footnote p. 1 of the draft Statute of this *Consilium*.

Velati notes aptly that the Secretariat was conceived as a sort of "alternative pole" to the Holy Office. And in fact in Vatican II *Bea's Secretariat* was in practice the counterpart of the Theological Commission, presided by Ottaviani, because it was the body that examined the ecumenical correctness of all the schemas to be presented in the council hall, that is, their conformity to the ecumenical directives imparted by John XXIII. Dogmatic correctness was thus contrasted – by a body willed by Pope Roncalli precisely for *this* purpose – by an ecumenical correctness, in fatal, strident contrast with the other body.

A two-faced body, or the disguised supercommission

The statute prepared by Bea in April 1960 *was never promulgated by the Pontiff.* After many years, scholars have found it in the Archives of the Second Vatican Council.[131] John XXIII expressly wanted the *Consilium* to assume the modest appearance of a "Secretariat". It was he who imposed the change of name to "Secretariat", when the new body was examined by the ante-preparatory commission of the Council, presided over by Cardinal Tardini.[132] This choice, comments Velati, "appeared at first very restrictive [for the Secretariat], effectively limiting the sphere of its competences and questioning its ability to participate in the actual preparatory work".[133] However, it was John XXIII who explained to Bea that the new body, presented in this way, "could move more freely in its assigned field, which was rather new and unusual".[134] In fact, as Velati notes, the motu proprio *Superno Dei Nutu*, which placed it among the Council's organs, presented it, as we have seen, "with a very brief reference that did not pretend to precisely identify the limits of the competence of the new Secretariat".[135] Angelo Roncalli then declared that he had wished to maintain the attribution of powers and competences in general terms: "These are the lines of our 'motu proprio': intentionally generic lines,

---

131 Ibid., p. 104.
132 Ibid., p. 116.
133 Ibid.
134 Ibid., p. 117. The statement is from Cardinal Bea.
135 Ibid.

which will allow for appropriate additions and extensions...".[136] These statements certainly did not prevent individuals from noticing some oddities or disproportions: instead of a simple prelate (as was the custom), the Secretariat had at its head a cardinal and manifested the explicitly declared structure of a commission: "and it will be constituted in the same way as the Commissions mentioned above".[137]

Bea's Secretariat was therefore a two-faced body. Officially, its functions were only to establish contacts of various kinds with the "separated brothers". In substance, however, it was from the very moment of its establishment a *disguised conciliar commission!* Its action took its inspiration from the principles of the Statute kept secret by the Pope. It was therefore an anomalous and peculiar commission. *Anomalous* compared to the Council regulations, since it did not contain members elected by the assembly; peculiar, because it acted as a sort of "supercommission" tasked with exercising an ideological censorship (where the "ideology" was the "ecumenism" professed by John XXIII) in relation to the work of all the other commissions and at the same time with preparing schemas that essentially covered all the vital themes of the Council. This is evident from the arguments of the *ten subcommittees* in which this fake "Secretariat" was articulated. They are: *1) De membris Ecclesiae; 2) De structura hierarchicae Ecclesiae; 3) De oecumenismo catholico et de opere conversionum; 4) De laicatu et tolerantia; 5) De Verbo Dei; 6) De quaestionibus liturgicis; 7) De matrimoniis mixtis; 8) De necessitate orationis maxime in temporibus nostris; 9) Problema oecumenicum centrale secundum orientationem hodiernam Consilii Oecumenici Genevensis; 10) Quaestiones de Judeis.*[138]

The dutiful resistance of Ottaviani and Tromp

At the end of his accurate essay, Velati offers this consideration: the vague attribution of the powers of the Secretariat "subsequently allowed some members of the Theological Commission to maintain

---

[136] Ibid.

[137] *Superno Dei Nutu*, cit., AAS, LII (1960), p. 436: "... *peculiaris Coetus seu Secretariatus instituitur, qui moderatorem habebit unum ex S.R.E. Cardinalibus, Nobis deligendum, eodemque modo ut Commissiones supra memoratae constituetur*".

[138] M. VELATI, *La proposta ecumenica del Segretariato per l'unità dei Cristiani*, op. cit., p. 280.

that the Secretariat had no right to participate directly in the
preparation of the Council, being only an informative body. This is
evidently an interpretation that is far from the real intentions of John
XXIII, who subsequently did not fail to support all the work of the
Secretariat".[139] In fact, in the diary of Fr. Tromp, secretary of the
Theological Commission, we read: "February 23, 1961. This morning
Msgr. Willebrands [secretary of the Secretariat] came. He wants a
mixed commission on the hierarchical nature of the Church, on the
members of the Church and on the laity in the Church [...] I told him
that the mixed commission is impossible because it cannot be done
with a "Secretariat". And then there should be no mixed commission
on purely dogmatic questions, because they belong solely to the
Theological Commission. But if the "Secretariat" wants to give an
opinion it will be received willingly, or if it wants to have friendly
conversations".[140]

According to the historiography of the modernizers, Ottaviani and
Tromp, instead, should have understood the *true intentions* of John
XXIII: their persistent refusal to acknowledge in the Secretariat the
rights of a real commission should be considered merely a "forced
interpretation". One of the members of Bea's Secretariat, Emile de
Smedt, Bishop of Bruges, with theatrical tones, during the dramatic
debate on *De Fontibus* even accused Ottaviani of disloyalty to the
Council, because the impasse to which the discussion had come – he
shouted from the podium – was due to the Cardinal's persistent
refusal to form a mixed commission in order to review the schema,
manifestly devoid of "ecumenical spirit".[141]

---

[139] M. VELATI, *"Un indirizzo a Roma"*, op. cit., p. 118.

[140] Quoted in M.-D. CHENU, *Diario*, op. cit., p. 123 n. 160.

[141] R.M. WILTGEN, p. 123. It is worth mentioning what Chenu noted in
this regard, on November 27, 1962: "Fr. Congar recalls the intervention in
which Msgr. De Smedt (Bruges) has publicly disclosed Ottaviani's
permanent rejection of any collaboration with the other commissions
during the preparatory work. This closed stance by Ottaviani has shocked
the Americans, sensitized to the fair play of the assemblies; this helped to
determine their vote against Ottaviani's schemas" (M.-D. CHENU, p. 123).
This "fair play" was in reality *unfair*, but "the Americans" evidently did not
understand it.

Cardinal Ottaviani had not really been guilty of any disloyalty. He and Fr. Tromp had done nothing but dutifully defend *the autonomy and the competence* of the Theological Commission – composed of distinguished scholars – which alone, according to the regulations and healthy theology, was responsible for the delicate task of elaborating the schema of the dogmatic texts concerning doctrine and therefore the deposit of faith. The embrace of extraneous elements, driven by an objective that was not that of defending dogma, and sometimes lacking the necessary expertise, would certainly have led to documents lacking clarity, and undermined by ambiguities and errors: which is precisely what happened. With the mixed commission, the institutionally *incompetent* body (the Secretariat) would have effectively controlled the institutionally *competent* body, subjecting it, as we said, to an *ideological* censorship!

The point of view of the Theological Commission was expressed with the utmost clarity during the preparatory phase. "The constitution on the Church has been drafted by order of the Sovereign Pontiff by the Theological Commission which, according to the indication of the Holy Father, is the only authoritative body in dogmatic matters. For this reason, if the other commissions are faced with points concerning doctrine or theology, they are subject to the power of revision enjoyed by the Theological Commission. For the same reason, the Theological Commission has never formed a mixed commission with the other commissions: a mixed commission implies, in fact, a shared authority on the same subject [...] Therefore, if the Theological Commission cannot form a mixed commission with the other commissions, which are set up for the examination of the schemas, it cannot form a commission with the Secretariats, whose responsibilities are outside the scope of the aforementioned examination". In this way, during the discussion on the *De Ecclesia* schema, in the preliminary phase, Cardinal Ottaviani responded to Cardinal Bea's criticisms, presented at the beginning of this paragraph.[142]

As all can see, it is a canonically and theologically irreproachable answer. It must then be stressed that it was not the task of the

---

[142] We have retranslated the passage from the French version of PH. LEVILLAIN, p. 255.

Theological Commission to read between the lines of John XXIII's
decrees (invisibile ones included) and take responsibility for resolving
the *willful ambiguities* in the sense desired by him, ambiguities placed
moreover at the service of a design dangerous for the faith.

The secret "manoeuvres" of John XXIII

From what has been seen so far, it can certainly be said that the
authority with which Cardinal Bea criticized the *De Ecclesia* schema
came from the Statute secretly approved by Pope Roncalli, the statute
of a conciliar commission, and not of a mere Secretariat. It was given
him, therefore, secretly, but directly, by John XXIII.

On October 15, 1962, Cardinal Bea addressed a letter, not to the
Presidency of the Council, but to Cardinal Amleto Cicognani as
President of the *Commission for Extraordinary Matters*, informing him
that on the next day (the 16th or 17th), it would receive more powers
with the papal rescript mentioned above (*this too kept secret*). In Bea's
letter, his Secretariat actually presented itself as the body charged with
pressing for the purposes openly willed by the Pope to be
accomplished in the Council, which he cited through numerous
references to the famous Opening Allocution.[143]

A week later, on October 22, 1962, with a rescript dated October
19, 1962, the Secretariat was officially installed by John XXIII in the
Council as a commission, a full two and a half years after the secret
approval of its statute. Fr. Wiltgen comments: "By not revealing his
decision [to have constituted this commission], the Pope had in fact
kept intact the group of representative personalities in the ecumenical
field, gathered by Cardinal Bea two years before. The Secretariat was
the only 'commission' not to have sixteen elected members".[144]

And this was undoubtedly, as we have said, its main anomaly. Not
such, we believe, to be considered invalid in its installation (or better,
unveiling) in the Council, since it certainly fell within the powers of the

---

[143] G. ALBERIGO, *Concilio acefalo?*, op. cit., pp. 196-197. The text of the
letter is published in Appendix I of the essay by Alberigo, pp. 219-224.
According to this historian, Bea's letter should be linked to the enlargement
of the powers of the Commission for extraordinary matters, immediately
following it.
[144] R.M. WILTGEN, p. 123.

Pope to perform such an act. However, John XXIII publicly sanctioned the existence of a commission which had been officially secret until then and which did not meet the requirements laid down by the Council regulations. In order to comply with the regulations (and therefore with the principle of legality), the Pope should have dissolved the Secretariat and re-presented its members to the Conciliar Assembly so that the latter could elect them in a new commission, for the matters pertaining to it. This is the least that should have been done by a Pope who really wanted to respect the so-called "freedom of the Council".

The decisive activity of the ecumenical supercommission

The careful reconstruction of the facts shows that Bea's Secretariat was conceived by John XXIII as a sort of *personal body of government of the Prince*, a direct and faithful emanation of the executive power, charged with scrupulously implementing his directives without the inconvenience of external influences. To better guarantee its action, Pope Roncalli made use of secrecy and a cleverly orchestrated ambiguity. John XXIII came from a long tenure in the diplomatic corps. He showed that he could apply, with cunning and iron determination, the ancient and refined techniques of *secret diplomacy*. But perhaps this was not all he used. Continuing our comparison with the French Revolution, the insidious action of the Secretariat in some respects evokes that of the "inner circles" of Freemasonry in guiding assemblies and votes, especially in the initial phase of the revolution, as emphasized by the classic studies of Auguste Cochin.[145]

---

[145] AUGUSTE COCHIN, "How the Deputies Were Elected to the States General", in *Organizing the Revolution: Selections from Auguste Cochin*, Chronicles Press, 2007, pp. 97-105. A further disconcerting aspect of the personality of John XXIII appears from his repeated affirmation, echoed by the very beginning of the Apostolic Letter *Superno Dei Nutu*, with which he established the preparatory commissions, according to which the Council was decided by him following a sudden inspiration from on High, which took place on 20 January 1958 during a meeting with the then Secretary of State, Msgr. Tardini: "*Superno Dei nutu factum esse reputavimus quod Nobis, ad Pontificale Solium vix evectis, Concilii Oecumenici celebrandi, veluti flos inexspectati veris, subiit cogitatio…*". The Pope's statements on this point were in fact

The Secretariat carried out decisive "ecumenical" activity during the two years of its life before the Council. It certainly took part, with some of its exponents, in the secret agreements that led to the Council's failure to condemn communism.[146] It was always a very faithful executor of Pope Roncalli's orders, even enduring (without batting an eye) scorching humiliations, such as that inflicted by the Patriarch of Moscow, who said he was willing to accept an invitation to the Council, only if it were personally delivered in Moscow by Msgr. Willebrands. The Pope authorized the prelate to do so, and so he arrived with a verbal invitation, which however was not accepted, as the Patriarch wanted a written one.[147]

For what concerns the Secretariat's activity as a conciliar committee, already in 1960 John XXIII had conferred on Bea the task

---

contradicted by various testimonies, including those of Cardinal Poupard (at the time Monsignor) and of Msgr. Capovilla, secretary of John XXIII. Even Levillain, an author perfectly aligned with the new direction, writes, quoting the very same Cardinal Poupard, that the convocation of an Ecumenical Council had already been decided well before the date of the presumed "inspiration" and already constituted "*un secret de comédie*", an open secret (PH. LEVILLAIN, p. 34 n. 2).

[146] R. AMERIO, § 38 (pp. 65-67).

[147] The written invitation was sent immediately afterwards. The story is recounted by R.M. WILTGEN, p. 122. On that occasion, Msgr. Willebrands stayed in Moscow for five days (September 27-October 2, 1962), an unusually long visit for a Western diplomat, albeit *sui generis*, in those times of strict "cold war" between the West and Communist Russia. The agreement between Rome and Moscow to avoid the condemnation of communism at the Council has been defined as the fruit of a completely unfounded rumor by the author of the third chapter of first volume of *Storia del Concilio Vaticano II*, p. 348. According to him, such an agreement never existed and the information recounted by Amerio is false. But Amerio based his work on accurate data which appeared not only in two well-known French Catholic newspapers but also in *France nouvelle* in its January 16-22, 1963 issue; this was the main bulletin of the French Communist Party (see R. AMERIO, § 38, [p. 66]). The existence of the agreement, respected in ironclad fashion by the Vatican, is confirmed by further, incontrovertible documentation. See, for the whole question, the accurate reconstruction by R. DE MATTEI, chap. VI § 9: *Il Concilio e il comunismo: storia di una mancata condanna*, pp. 492-504.

of preparing a schema on "freedom of worship", afterwards merged with that on "religious freedom", and a special schema on the Jews (in the private audience of September 18, 1960), a schema which later merged (in modified form) into the Conciliar Declaration *Nostra Aetate*[148]. In the Council, the Secretariat did not limit itself to incorporate the activity of the Theological Commission: it proposed in the council hall the schema on ecumenism, that on non-Christian religions and finally that on religious freedom, this last schema being the most fought-over of the whole Council, revised a full six times.[149] All these schemas concerned topics that were particularly dear to Angelo Roncalli, an ancient fellow disciple of Ernesto Buonaiuti, his fraternal friend at the Roman Seminary and himself suspected of modernism by the ecclesiastical authority of that time: topics which particularly characterized the peculiar conception of ecumenism held by "good Pope John".

---

[148] R.M. WILTGEN, pp. 160-161; p. 167.
[149] Ibid., p. 53, p. 126, p. 167 ff; pp. 160-161.

7.

DEI VERBUM, THE FRUIT OF THE "PARALLEL COUNCIL": A SYNOPSIS OF ITS TORTUOUS AND CONTESTED ITER IN AULA

A legal fiction

Let's now return to the discussion in the council hall on the *De Fontibus Revelationis* schema. We have seen that John XXIII, renouncing the application of the regulations made by the Presidency of the Council, interrupted, once again in an informal way, that is, "*vivae vocis oraculo*", the discussion itself and entrusted the revision of the schema to a mixed commission formed by members of the Theological Commission (the only competent body in the matter) and members of the Secretariat for Christian Unity (whose competence was not apparent, except to direct the revision of the schema according to the "ecumenical" sense desired by the Pope). We have also seen that the aforementioned schema was immediately rebaptized *De Divina Revelatione*, as if to indicate that the wind was blowing now in the direction of the novators of the European Alliance, who, after the manner of the Protestants and against the whole Tradition of the Church, did not want to hear talk of two sources of Revelation (Sacred Scripture and Tradition).

The *mixed* character of the new commission, charged with reworking the schema under this new name, was in fact a *legal fiction* that concealed the total control of the Secretariat for the promotion of Christian unity, presided by Bea, over the works of the Theological Commission presided by Ottaviani. In fact, the "mixed" work was normally carried out as follows: the Theological Commission was divided into sub-commissions, composed of Fathers and experts, who carried out their revision of the text; the texts were subsequently sent to the Secretariat (i.e., to Bea), who approved them if he found them to his liking; otherwise, the Secretariat would request a joint meeting with the Theological Commission to discuss the necessary changes.[150]

However, it would still be a long battle for the novators. To triumph, they would have to increase their numbers in the same Theological Commission and benefit from the reform of the Council Regulations, begun by John XXIII and completed by Paul VI on September 13, 1963.

A permanent climate of confusion and of uncertain legality

It is necessary to dedicate a few words to this aspect of the Council. Vatican II was constituted by an assembly of almost 2,500 people: a gigantic dimension, which posed complex organizational problems. But the merely technical problems (streamlining the work, avoiding delays and repetitions, and reforming via praxis the organs charged with directing the debate) were intertwined with questions of substance, which the technical problems served instead to mask, since *the real confrontation was a doctrinal one*. If there had been agreement on doctrine, the whole Council would have lasted a few months.

As we have seen, John XXIII initiated the reform of the regulations, first de facto and then according to law. He did so de facto, with the oblique strategy we have described, consisting of secretly granting wider powers to the *Secretariat for Extraordinary Affairs*. He did so according to law, by subsequently establishing the *Coordination Commission*, which was supposed to coordinate the work, also exercising control over the texts prepared by the Commissions before they were presented in the council hall.

We must not believe that with this the climate of confusion and of uncertain legality completely disappeared. On closer inspection, it characterized the course of the Council until the end. The confusion could not have ceased, also because John XXIII had multiplied the centers of initiative, inviting, as we have seen, even the Episcopal Conferences to participate in the re-elaboration of the schemas during the intersession. This allowed the European Alliance to present itself at the beginning of the second session with alternative

---

[150] For this reconstruction see R.M. WILTGEN, pp. 176-177. The "special and mixed" subcommittees, as will be recalled, were introduced by John XXIII to break the hegemony of the Roman Curia.

texts to those of the commissions; in particular with a new *De Ecclesia* schema, whose first words were: *Lumen Gentium.*[151]

The reform of the regulations later carried out by Paul VI only made adjustments, albeit essential ones. The *Presidency of the Council* was brought from ten to twelve cardinals and at the same time was definitively deprived of any effective power of direction over the Assembly, entrusted instead to a college of four moderating cardinals, who governed the assembly as the Pope's legates. These cardinals were not drawn from the Presidency but from the *Coordination Commission* (whose members were brought to nine), to which the Moderators continued to belong. This expansion of the list did not prevent Paul VI from manoeuvering so as to give the novators *absolute control* over the *College of Moderators,* since it was composed of Döpfner, Suenens, Lercaro and Agagianian: only the latter was not part of the European Alliance. The *Secretariat for Extraordinary Matters* was abolished. Following these reforms, there were now a full *three* governing bodies, with a situation of potential and permanent conflict between the two that actually counted: the *Coordination Commission* (whose secretary was now also secretary of the Council) and the *College of the (four) Moderators.*[152]

The lack of an effective institutional clarity did not prevent but rather facilitated the emergence of the brutal strategy of the novators, supported by Paul VI, and whose aim was *pure and simple control of the majority* in the commissions and in the governing bodies of the Council.

The reform of the regulations then obligatorily introduced theologians as experts (or *consultores*) into the commissions and allowed lay experts to be admitted under certain conditions. The principle of the qualified (two-thirds) majority was maintained for the approval of the schemas or their parts or amendments; for their rejection or postponement, however, a simple majority was declared sufficient. A new schema or an organic set of amendments could be presented in the council hall to the Moderator, provided they were supported by at least fifty Fathers. The Moderator would then send

---

[151] R.M. WILTGEN, p. 58, p. 64.

[152] PH. LEVILLAIN, pp. 299-313; G. ALBERIGO, *Dinamiche e procedure nel Vaticano II,* op. cit., passim; ID., *Concilio acefalo?,* op. cit., pp. 205-217.

them to the *Coordination Commission*, which would decide what to do with them.[153]

The "compromises"

The component of the Theological Commission still faithful to dogma defended its positions tenaciously. Cardinal Ottaviani, originally from a humble family of the old Catholic Rome, fought like a lion. His opponents themselves had to acknowledge it.[154]

The revised text of the *De Divina Revelatione* schema was distributed to the Fathers in May 1963, but the novators did not like it. Therefore, in August of the same year, the bishop of Eichstätt, Msgr. Schröffer, a member of the Theological Commission and a man of modernizing tendencies, in his report to the Fathers of the German-speaking European Alliance, who were about to meet in Germany (at the Fulda Conference), wrote that the revised schema showed itself to be "the result of a laborious battle", so as to constitute "a compromise, with all the disadvantages of compromises". And not only that: the prelate expressed his pessimism about the possibility of obtaining anything more. He enclosed with his letter detailed observations on the schema, prepared by Karl Rahner, S.J. Rahner's comment was shared by Grillmeier, Semmelroth and Ratzinger.[155] But what did the novators mean by "compromise"? Simply the fact that they had not been able to impose their point of view, which was the one that adhered most to *ecumenism*. Here is one example. The dogma of the absolute inerrancy of the Sacred Scriptures could not be accepted as the *De Fontibus Revelationis* schema had reproposed it, based on the perennial teaching of the Church: the Protestants would have taken it badly. However, the resistance of the "conservatives" had to be taken into account. Therefore, in the text published by the mixed commission, Msgr. Spadafora noted, "all doubts about the absolute inerrancy of Sacred Scripture are excluded: 'Since God', it is written, 'is affirmed to be and is the principal author of the whole of Scripture, it follows that the whole of Scripture, as divinely inspired, is immune from all error'. In this text, which replaced the original, there is only

---

153 PH. LEVILLAIN, pp. 299-304.
154 Ibid., pp. 81-82.
155 For all these details see R.M. WILTGEN, pp. 175-176.

a small warning signal: the term 'inerrancy' has disappeared from the title of the relevant chapter. It no longer reads '*De Sacrae Scripturae inspiratione, inerrantia et compositione litteraria*', but: '*De Sacrae Scripturae inspiratione et interpretatione*'. This is only the beginning...".[156]

The conquest of the Theological Commission

The Fulda Conference, adopting Karl Rahner's viewpoint, officially asked that the *De Divina Revelatione* schema not be discussed at the beginning of the second session. Cardinal Döpfner made a useful contribution by participating on August 31, 1963 in a meeting of the *Coordination Commission*, of which he was a member and which was to decide the work calendar, and the discussion of the disputed schema was moved to the beginning of the third session.

In December 1963, at the end of the second session, which began the previous September, with Paul VI already reigning, the Theological Commission received four new members, all belonging to the European Alliance, and thus to the modernizing wing. At the same time, the Fathers were allowed to send "*emendationes*", written amendments on the schema until January 31, 1964.[157] In this way the novators had for the first time a majority in the Theological Commission.

It was only after these appointments and only after the Theological Commission was subdivided into the subcommittees mentioned above, with broad input of the Fathers and experts of "modernizing" or pro-modernizing tendencies (we recall Msgr. Charue, Bishop of Namur, Msgr. Dodewaard, Bishop of Haarlem, the Archbishop of Florence, Msgr. Ermenegildo Florit; the theologians Grillmeier, Semmelroth, Rahner, Congar etc.), that the Coordination Commission invited the Theological Commission to proceed with the revision of the schema.[158] We can well say that the fragmentation into sub-commissions, in which the novators were very well represented,

---

[156] F. SPADAFORA, *La 'Nuova Esegesi'*, op. cit., p. 161. The Author offers the original Latin in a footnote.

[157] For this reconstruction of the facts, we rely on R.M. WILTGEN, p. 176.

[158] Ibid.

constituted the last phase of the long war started by John XXIII against the Theological Commission and continued by his successor.

Nothing left to chance

Some observations are necessary.

The text revised during the work of the intersession (December 1962 – September 1963) and prepared by the "mixed" commission should have been discussed in the council hall during the second session of the council's work. Instead the discussion was postponed to the third session. In this way the novators had time to modify it further through the subcommittees filled with theologians to their liking and whose participation in the works was made possible by the reform of the Council regulations, which entered into force at the beginning of the second session, September 1963.

These further modifications, however, do not appear to be at all proper from a procedural point of view, since they were made to a text that had not been discussed in the council hall in its various parts. To respect the so-called "freedom of the Council" they should have been introduced only after having presented the revised text in the hall during the intersession, so as to take into account the possible observations expressed by the Council Fathers. Instead, the text initially elaborated by the mixed commission (and unwelcome to the progressives) did not reach the council hall in the end, but rather the further revision of the text that the subcommittees had carried out. That is, what reached the council hall was a text twice revised, and the second time in accordance with the request of the Fulda Conference, which was deployed in formation behind the positions of Karl Rahner and his companions, and only after the addition of four new members gave the novators a majority in the Theological Commission. As one can see, nothing was left to chance. It is true that the Fathers were authorized to send written *emendationes* until the end of January 1964; it was, however, a modest substitute for free discussion in the assembly.

The path of the new schema

Let us now follow the further development of *De Divina Revelatione*, again based on Fr. Wiltgen's reconstruction, which we find reliable and trustworthy.

The experts of the sub-commissions concluded their work on April 24, 1964 and sent their texts to Bea's Secretariat for approval. The following May 30, the latter gave its approval, declaring that a joint meeting with the Theological Commission was not necessary.[159] The Secretariat therefore approved the text prepared by the sub-commissions. One of these, presided over by the aforementioned Msgr. Dodewaard, was responsible, it was later realized, for having introduced into the text a real heresy, that of the *"veritas salutaris"* as the only truth actually taught without error in the Scriptures. *This was a heresy*, because it implicitly denied the dogma of the inerrancy of all of Scripture, even in things not directly concerning the faith. But let us proceed with order.

After the approval by the Secretariat, the entire Theological Commission held four meetings, from June 3-5, 1964, evidently without making further modifications (otherwise they should have been submitted to the Secretariat, inaugurating the process described above). The text was then sent to the Coordination Commission, which approved it. The Pope's approval, "as a basis for discussion" came on July 3.[160] Two weeks after the opening of the third session, the schema was finally presented in the hall by Archbishop Florit on September 30, 1964. Of the original text, proposed at the time by Ottaviani and rejected (as we have seen) without its being discussed, little was left. The novators now dominated the situation, so much so that the schema was not presented by Cardinal Ottaviani, although he was always formally the President of the Theological Commission. The schema was discussed for five days. The debate ended on October 6, 1964. The Theological Commission re-examined everything that had been said orally and put in writing during the debate and on November 20, 1964, the last meeting of the session, it

---

[159] Ibid., pp. 176-177.
[160] Ibid.

gave the Fathers "the new draft of the schema". They could propose further observations in writing until January 31, 1965.

The *Coetus Internationalis Patrum*, which numbered almost three hundred bishops faithful to Tradition (they had had to form an organization as well, albeit a rudimentary one compared to that of the rich European Alliance), sent to its members an eleven-page document with a letter, which stated that the approval of the schema was conditional on the acceptance of some essential changes, concerning inter alia the articles 9, 11, and 19. The Theological Commission, however, did not want to make any changes, and for that matter it was not legally obliged to accept any amendment, as such.[161]

The voting took place at the beginning of the fourth session (September 20-25, 1965). According to Fr. Wiltgen, *a clear violation of the procedure occurred here*. In fact, the regulations (art. 61 § 3) required that a member of the Theological Commission make a report to the Fathers on the text before the vote, but this did not take place.[162] There were six votes, one for each part of the schema. Each part was approved with a majority even greater than two-thirds, required by the regulations. A part of the favorable votes had been given "*iuxta modum*", i.e., requiring modifications, in particular to the aforementioned articles 9, 11, and 19. But the Commission refused to change anything, taking refuge behind the argument that the texts had been approved by a majority even greater than two-thirds of the votes required by the regulations. The principle of a qualified majority, judged two years before by the novators to be "a weak point in the procedure" (see above), now became agreeable to them, allowing them to hole up in the advantageous positions they had patiently reached.

The Commission's argument was formally legitimate, but in reality it was misleading because the favorable vote of a majority, albeit a qualified one, did not invalidate the Commission's faculty of accepting amendments attached to a part of those votes, a part which for that matter constituted a portion of the majority. If it had wanted,

---

[161] Ibid., p. 178.

[162] Ibid. The violation was evidently tolerated by the cardinal moderator who directed the debate in the hall.

the Commission could have accepted them without violating the regulations in any way. (Conversely, in the case already extensively illustrated above of the violation of conciliar legality of November 21, 1962, the failure to reach the quorum of two-thirds of the votes on the proposal to interrupt the discussion entailed a single legitimate legal consequence, pursuant to the regulations: the *obligation* to continue the debate).

Very serious criticism and an obligatory intervention by Paul VI

The criticism of the *Coetus Internationalis Patrum* and other "conservative" bishops concerned above all articles 9, 11, and 19 of *Dei Verbum*. They contained serious ambiguities in relation to the concept of Tradition and its relationship with the Holy Scriptures (art. 9); they did not clearly confirm the dogma of divine and Catholic faith of the inerrancy of the Sacred Scriptures, but rather (as we said) they opened the door to a real heresy, insinuating that Sacred Scripture teaches with certainty and truth the only "saving truth" (*Veritas salutaris*) (art. 11); they did not give a clear idea of the historicity of the Gospels, hiding in the text the erroneous and fatal theses of the so-called "historical-critical method" (art. 19). All this undermined the deposit of faith.

The Theological Commission, however, did not abandon its positions, thanks to the modernizing majority that had emerged within it, which succeeded in imposing its point of view in all the internal votes called in order to accommodate the changes requested. The progressives continued to state that a text approved by more than two-thirds of the Fathers could not be changed, but it must be remembered that they had succeeded in imposing the rejection of any change even before the vote: the will to make their text prevail at any cost was therefore already evident well before the vote.

The situation was scandalous. Consequently, the bishops faithful to Tradition exerted a strong pressure on the Pope to intervene with his authority before the final vote on the schema in public session.[163] After having consulted with Cardinal Bea and the four Moderators,

---

[163] Ibid., p. 180; F. SPADAFORA, *La 'Nuova Esegesi'*, p. 164.

Paul VI decided to exercise his powers, that is, to reconvene the Theological Commission, "not to alter", he wrote, "the schema or the work of the Commission but to improve it in some points of great doctrinal importance". He wanted Cardinal Bea "to be invited to the meeting of the Theological Commission", during which his letter was read, containing the directives for resolving the thorny passages.[164] The solutions eventually adopted, after meticulous debate, were therefore those chosen by the Commission with Bea's approval and partly coincided with the papal suggestions.

Regarding the "*veritas salutaris*", Bea noted that the passage had not been approved at a meeting of the mixed commission, but had been added later.[165] This made it legitimate to delete it from the text (it was possible to remove it only on the basis of this legal observation). The amendments (to be precise one in art. 11 and two additions to the text) were subsequently approved on October 29, 1965, while the final public vote took place on November 18, 1965. There were only six *non-placets* out of 2,350 voters.[166] In reality it was a *compromise solution* that did not definitively solve the problems. The modified passage of art. 11 reads: "[...] it is necessary, therefore, to hold that the books of Scripture teach with certainty, faithfully and without error, the truth that God, for our salvation, wanted to be delivered in the Sacred Scriptures". It is clear that this text can still allow, for those who so desire, the heterodox interpretation according to which the truth that is taught in the Holy Scriptures "without error" is solely that which concerns "our salvation".[167]

---

[164] R.M. WILTGEN, p. 181.

[165] Ibid., pp. 182-183. The person in charge of the coup seems to have been the Dutch Msgr. Jan van Dodewaard, bishop of Haarlem, president of the subcommittee dealing with the chapters of the schema concerning the Holy Scriptures (for an accurate reconstruction of the misdeed, see F. SPADAFORA, op. cit., p. 160 ff. Msgr. Spadafora, a prominent exegete, was asked to send a brief opinion to the Commission containing the true doctrine of the Church on the matter; this opinion was forwarded to the Pope through Cardinal Browne, vice-president of the Theological Commission – Ibid., p. 164).

[166] R.M. WILTGEN, p. 183.

[167] For the text of the Council in Italian, see *I DOCUMENTI DEL CONCILIO VATICANO II. Costituzioni – Decreti – Dichiarazioni*, Edizioni

The rebirth of modernism

On this sad and unheard-of affair we wish to note the following.

The legitimate president of the Theological Commission was always Cardinal Ottaviani, but Paul VI wanted Cardinal Bea *to preside* over the Commission's rescheduling session. With this extraordinary "presidency" we can say that Bea also symbolically won a victory against Ottaviani, the *defensor fidei*. But it was a Pyrrhic victory because the tremendous responsibility, before God and the faithful, of having accepted, with the permission of the Pope, a compromise solution on serious matters of faith weighed and still weighs on him, as well as on Paul VI.

Concerning the surreptitious insertion of the phrase on "saving truth", we ask at what point in the complicated development of the schema did it take place. Perhaps when the Theological Commission reviewed all the observations of the Fathers and prepared the schema that was then put to a vote without ever being presented again to Bea's Secretariat for examination? But should not the schema, before being put to a vote, have been examined by the *Coordination Committee*, composed, as one will recall, of nine cardinals and presided by the Pope? In short: how was it possible for a text that contained a statement so openly inclined to heresy to obtain the final approval that immediately preceded the public vote? This very serious fact demonstrates the inefficiency of the Council's governing bodies and the confusion that prevailed in it (and confusion, we know, does not come from the Holy Spirit). Moreover, it shows that Ottaviani's and Tromp's aversion towards the mixed commissions, especially in the doctrinal field, was perfectly justified: even unwittingly, such commissions favored procedural messes and surprise manoeuvres.

One might be surprised to observe the tenacity shown by the novators in defending their texts, even in the face of open requests for amendments that the Pope eventually had to make. In this

---

Paoline, 1980, p. 159. For the original in Latin: *CONCILII OECUMENICI VATICANI II. Constitutiones – Decreta – Declarationes*, Desclée ac Socii, Romae 1967, p. 9: *"Cum ergo omne id, quod auctores inspirati seu hagiographi asserunt, retineri debeat assertum a Spiritu Sancto, inde Scripturae libri veritatem, quam Deus nostrae salutis causa Litteris Sacris consignari voluit, firmiter, fideliter et sine errore docere profitendi sunt"*.

resistance to the bitter end we see a proof of the loss of prestige of the papacy as an institution, caused by the oblique politics of John XXIII, as amply illustrated above; this loss was accentuated under Paul VI, who cemented the unprecedented image of the Supreme Pontiff as one who on the one hand served merely as the Council's notary and on the other acted as a simple referee between the sides.

It should also be remembered that for de Lubac *Dei Verbum* was "the most important and decisive expression of the whole Council".[168] The "new theologians", actively present in the final drafting of the text, knew perfectly well that the Protestant corruption of the sources of Revelation, sanctioned by an Ecumenical Council, even one that was *merely pastoral*, would fatally penetrate the Pontifical Universities and seminaries, eventually corrupting the faith of the priests and believers, so as to subject them, defenseless, to the assault of contemporary thought and mentality, of which they were admirers and disciples (some of them even reflecting this admiration in their daily lives).

There is no doubt, as Etienne Fouilloux has said, that with the rejection of the *De Fontibus Revelationis* schema, the stage of the anti-modernist reaction truly comes to an end.[169] And the same is true (see above) for the *Catholic Counter-Reformation*, which was, thanks to the dogmatic Council of Trent, the true reform of the Church, against the schisms and the terrible heresies of the Protestants.

This has resulted in nothing less than the resurgence of modernism like a phoenix from the ashes of that healthy "Roman intransigence" allowed to fall completely and culpably into nothingness by "the good Pope John".

---

[168] KARL-HEINZ NEUFELD S.J., *Vescovi e teologi al servizio del Concilio Vaticano II*, in RENÉ LATOURELLE (Ed.), *Vaticano II: Bilancio e prospettive. Venticinque anni dopo (1962-1987)*, Cittadella ed., Assisi 1987, pp. 83-109; p. 101.

[169] Cfr. "Sì sì no no", March 31, 2000, p. 2.

TABLE OF CONTENTS

www.ingramcontent.com/pod-product-compliance
Lightning Source LLC
Chambersburg PA
CBHW032024090426
42741CB00006B/725